PICASSO
LITHOGRAPHS

FERNAND MOURLOT

BOSTON BOOK AND ART PUBLISHER

TRANSLATED FROM THE FRENCH BY JEAN DIDRY

LIBRARY OF CONGRESS CATALOG CARD NUMBER 70-129449

© ANDRÉ SAURET · ÉDITIONS DU LIVRE
© PICASSO 1970 BY S.P.A.D.E.M., PARIS

PRINTED IN FRANCE

PICASSO'S IRON WALL

Hélène Parmelin

The artist never submits to his material; he makes it the instrument of his will.
Prehistoric man facing the wall of his cave, Goya or Daumier their lithographic stones,
Durer his copperplate, Michaelangelo the ceiling of the Sistine Chapel, Degas his linocuts,
Matisse his collages, and the many other great artists, have all been involved in the same
eternal quest. The material is the slave, not the master who imposes his laws and restrictions.
The artist remains a prey to the one irrational obsession that urges him ever on to express what
he and other men have seen, but not with the same eyes, and to imbue it with the magnetic
power of thought. He loads himself with work which, by a cumulative process, confers on
him a greater liberty: that of possessing an instrument, a tool, a way of being, a craft so finely
tempered that his hand lacks no skill. He knows. He knows immediately,
or perhaps he takes a long time to know; but from the moment that he knows this liberty,
there remains for him only the shadowy problem of the iron wall of which Van Gogh spoke:
"What is it to be an artist? How can one achieve the desired result? One has to pass through
the invisible iron wall that seems to stand between what one feels and what one is capable of.
How can one pass through this barrier? To cast oneself blindly against it achieves nothing.
To my mind one has to undermine, to file away at the wall, gradually, patiently..."
Nothing counts but this "invisible iron wall". What the artist wants to achieve;
what he does achieve; the innovative or the destructive effort.
And intimately linked with this difficulty is the desire to fulfil oneself, by producing from
one's very being something that has never before had existence. The wall of iron must be
crossed and to this victory must at times be added that of forcing a material to submit,
with the craftsman's joy in dominating and twisting the ancient laws.
A characteristic of Picasso is to question all definitions. Reality is not what we think it to be.

Provided we do not stop at mere superficial appearances the value of his life becomes multiplied tenfold. With his alert, ultra-sharp eye, his ever-receptive mind, Picasso is not a magician. He knows how to look into the very depths of people and of things. A pitcher cast aside by a potter becomes for him the teats of a she-goat, teats that surpass in their swollen, round abundance those of all the ancient goddesses of fertility. What unsuspecting palm tree produced the large leaf whose central vein now forms the most realistically spiny backbone for the she-goat under its casing of plaster? The whole, cast in bronze, becomes "The She-Goat" in all its verity. This is not a game: it is the great quest for reality. To create his she-goat Picasso crossed the iron wall a palm tree branch in his hand. Nowadays, when Fernand Mourlot speaks of Picasso the lithographer, he says, "He looked, he listened, he did the opposite of what he had learnt - and it worked." The potters of Ramié and Vallauris could say the same of the unexpected potter who descended upon them one fine day. "He did everything that we told him not to do," with the enamels, with glazes - and it worked. His engravers, the brothers Crommelynck, could repeat the same tale of the engraver who, with superb nochalance, broke all the strict rules of a difficult art. And, contrary to all expectations, it worked. But "it works", of course, because Picasso thinks, learns, assimilates, uses his hands, experiments, acquires the necessary skills and tries everything. Writing of Picasso's very first lithographs Sabartès said: "We can see from the first series of his lithographs that we know of, that whether using crayon or ink he tried to understand the real nature of lithography." Picasso, who has tried every method of transmitting a thought, is quite the opposite of the happy-go-lucky, try-anything type who can do anything with his hands, breaks all the rules and succeeds at the first attempt like the tyro gambler with his beginner's luck. And yet the phrase "he can do anything he wants with his hands" fits him like a glove. This is because he has a great respect for the craft, an insatiable curiosity about his material, and because his desire to cross the iron wall requires all the possible backing of technique that an artist can have in order to say what he has to say in the most truthful way. The story of the bull is an exceptional example of this. It happened at Mourlot's works in 1945, in the old workshops in Rue de Chabrol. I was told the story a few days ago by Jean Célestin, who was working with Picasso at the time, and who says of him: "He has left his mark on me .Working with Picasso has added something special to my life". And he adds: "He has a feeling; he has, how shall I put it, incredible talents... he is gifted; he is a painter.'' The story has two aspects; that of Picasso at work and that of Picasso faced by the iron wall, that Célestin expresses admirably.

It must be admitted that at Mourlot's he was awaited in the press shop with some scepticism.
How many painters pass and have passed through the shop. The workmen would watch them
at work, (I am speaking of those who made their own lithographs) and make their judgment.
"We gave him a stone and, two minutes later he was at work with crayon and brush.
And there was no stopping him. As lithographers we were astounded by him.
When you make a lithograph, the stone has been prepared, and if you have to make
a correction the stone has to be re-touched. ...Right. We run off 12 to 15 proofs for him and
return the stone to him in good order. Then he makes his second state.
On a stone like that, normally, when it has been retouched twice, the original preparation
becomes somewhat spoilt... And he would scrape and add ink and crayon and change
everything! After this sort of treatment the design generally becomes indecipherable
and is destroyed. But, with him! Each time it would turn out very well. Why? That's a mystery..."
Célestin says that Picasso is "a real hard worker". "We used to leave at 8 at night and he would
be there at 8.30 in the morning. Sometimes I would suggest that we should call it a day...
He would look at the stone, light up a Gauloise and give me one, and then we were off again...
Then at night at home he would make a litho on transfer paper on his kitchen stove
and in the morning we would start again". Henri Deschamps: "He would engrave the stone
with a scraper... the stone would be completely ravaged.
But we were so fond of him that he could have gone right through the stone!"
In between times, "we chatted and joked. But once work had started it was total concentration."
"It was a real passion" says Mourlot. And, with a detached air: "At that time, of course,
he did many engravings. But this did not prevent him from doing a lot of zincs for us as well..."
He adds: "When the old lithographers told him that they usually put a mask over their mouths
to prevent saliva spattering on the stone, he would laugh and answer:
"the saliva makes a blank, and we can make use of it..."
The story of the bull should be heard in the huge workshops, where the vats of ink shine,
the machines turn, posters are hung all about, the workmen bustle at their work
and the painters pass by. On the wall there is a poster for a Picasso exhibition at Avignon.
Mourlot's voice softens: "He is a friend and a man of extraordinary generosity.
But he is not prepared to accept the slightest retouching of his work. One day a crack appeared
in a small line. We put it right. After his very first glance Picasso said: "I didn't do that..."
We told him: "Yes, we put it right". "Oh", he replied, "You should not have done that."

And he was right. Every little thing is important. It changes nothing, yet it changes everything..."
And this is how the story of the bull ended:
"One day", said Célestin, "He started work on the famous bull. It was a superb,
well-rounded bull. I thought myself that that was that. But not at all.
A second state and a third state, still well-rounded, followed. And so it went on.
But the bull was no longer the same. It began to get smaller and to lose weight..."
That same day Deschamps told me that Picasso "was taking away rather than adding to his
composition... He was carving away slices of his bull at the same time.
And after each change we pulled a proof. He could see that we were puzzled.
He made a joke, he went on working, and then he produced another bull.
And each time less and less of the bull remained. He used to look at me and laugh.
"Look Henri," he would say, "we ought to give this bit to the butcher. The housewife could say:
I want that piece, or this one..." In the end, the bull's head was like that of an ant."
And to conclude the story of the bull Célestin said: "At the last proof there remained only
a few lines. I had watched him at work, reducing, always reducing.
I still remembered the first bull and I said to myself: What I don't understand is that he
has ended up where really he should have started! But he, Picasso, was seeking his own bull.
And to achieve his one line bull he had gone in successive stages through all the other bulls.
And when you look at that line you cannot imagine how much work it had involved..."
"There are paintings in which there seems to be nothing, yet which contain everything",·
said Corot. And the progression to the bull is typical of this. Each state has its meaning and
each of these meanings leads towards another form of truth. What remains carries all the
range of thought we imply when we say the word "bull".
And this is also one of the strengths of lithography, of engraving, of linocut.
In each of these art forms there are clear cut "states". The stages are clearly defined.
They are all there before one's eyes. For the onlooker it is a rare experience which only books
of lithographs or engravings can give. We see lines move, marks come and go,
changes everywhere. We follow the line of thought, we understand everything,
we understand nothing. We see the many faces of reality eliminated or multiplied tenfold.
We feel the churning of thought and something of the reality of painting comes through to us.
We feel that we are sharing in the painter's adventure.
We can reflect upon the heights and depths of creation...
On one occasion Picasso took part in some film-making. Or, more exactly, Picasso's painting

took an actor's part in the film "Le Mystère Picasso". In this film one could see part of the reality of the metamorphosis of a canvas into a painting. But there are no "states" in painting and each stage is superimposed on the next. The painter is carried forward with nothing to refer to and with no possibility of going back.

The artist is carried forward by his canvas and by himself and the canvas forms an implacable whole in which one "state" is inseparable from the next. Perhaps this is why painting is the artist's most redoubtable and most complete form of expression. Lithography calls for the same expenditure of creative energy, and involves the same tension. But, like engraving or ceramics, it includes also a certain aspect of craftsmanship which conditions the artist. Like painting it is an adventure. One can spoil a lithograph just as one can spoil a canvas. But there is no other resemblance. (Lithography is a process, painting is not).

And yet, said Deschamps, "we never liked showing him the first proof very much. He would come and sit on the frame of the hand press. And on days when he felt that what he had done had been a failure, he seemed almost to look paler..."

The fact is that all that can be said about the techniques involved does not really count. These are mere details. Whatever the creative tool used may be, the iron wall is everywhere the same. Picasso the lithographer is still just Picasso. In a given period, everything that sees the light of day is akin, whether on canvas, paper, stone, lino, zinc, or in plaster or earthenware. One day I asked Picasso what difference there was for him between lithography, linocut and engraving. He replied that, of course, they were not at all the same. The graving tool... The strips of lino that are cut away... (speaking of the lithographic crayon he said: "It is soft"). But what one is searching for in all of them, that is always the same thing.

Yet the famous blacks and whites of lithographs (as in those of engraving) have a special soul of their own. All the different types of blacks form one range of colours; the whites another. Blacks on whites or whites on blacks, the lines are made with a material that resembles nothing else. The glow of the whites is soft or flashing. The greys are so varied that they seem to contain within them all the colours in the world. Yes, there is a whole world in lithography in which the colours seem unlike any other colours, and to which the posters add a dazzling tone of life, gaiety, fantasy and inventiveness. Meanwhile Picasso still faces the iron wall of creation. He goes on searching as if he were himself the consecutive "states" of one of his lithographs. The work increases and the search intensifies with its proofs both on paper and of the soul. Herein lies all the mad folly and the great rationality of the creative act.

Before publishing reproductions of Picasso's
works produced since November 2nd, 1945,
we felt that we should present the lithographs
made by the artist between 1919 and 1930.
Through the courtesy of Mr. Bernhard Geiser,
who has been kind enough to let us have access
to some very rare proofs,
we have thus been able to cover
all Picasso's lithographic work.
We wish to express our most grateful thanks
to Doctor Geiser as well as to our friend
Henri Kahnweiler and Madame Louise Leiris
whose collaboration has been most valuable.

II. WOMAN SITTING IN FRONT OF A WINDOW

I. THE WINDOW AT SAINT-RAPHAEL

III. PORTRAIT OF RAYMOND RADIGUET

3

I. THE WINDOW AT SAINT-RAPHAEL

1919. Format 5-1/4" x 3-1/4" (13,2 x 8,4 cm).
Lithographic ink drawing on paper
transferred to stone.
Invitation card drawn for
the Paul Rosenberg exhibition
of drawings and aquarelles by Picasso,
October 20th, to November 15th, 1919.
Run of 1,500 copies on thin cardboard,
format of card 5-3/4" x 3-3/4" (14,3 x 9,2 cm.)
(B. Biberon, printer). Stone polished out.

II. WOMAN SITTING IN FRONT OF A WINDOW

1919.   Format 8-" x 6-3/4" (20 x 17 cm).
Lithographic ink drawing on paper
transferred to stone.
Lithograph made for the cover of a catalogue
for a Paul Rosenberg exhibition of drawings and
aquarelles by Picasso (October - November 1919).
Format of catalogue
10-1/2" x 8-1/4" (26,9 x 20,9 cm).
(B. Biberon, printer). Stone polished out.

III. PORTRAIT OF RAYMOND RADIGUET

December 17th, 1920.
Format 4-1/2" x 3-3/4" (11,5 x 9,8 cm).
Lithographic crayon drawing on transfer paper.
This drawing was not transferred;
it was reproduced by collotype process.
Frontispiece to "Les joues en feu",
("Rosy Cheeked"), by Raymond Radiguet.
Bernard Grasset, Publisher, 1925.
The drawing on paper has gone astray.

6/26

V. PORTRAIT OF PAUL VALERY   VI. PORTRAIT OF PAUL VALERY

VII. THREE HORSES BY THE SEA

IV. PORTRAIT OF PAUL VALERY

4

IV. PORTRAIT OF PAUL VALERY

1920. Format of book 7"x5" (18x13 cm).
Lithographic crayon drawing on paper
transferred to stone.
A few trial proofs on different types of paper.
Run of 525 proofs on Arches laid paper,
unsigned and not numbered. Frontispiece to
"La jeune Parque" ("The Young Parque"),
by Paul Valéry. Nouvelle Revue Française, 1921.
(Marchizet, printer). Stone polished out.

V and VI. PORTRAITS OF PAUL VALERY

1920. Crayon drawing on paper transferred to stone.
Transfer effected by Pitault in 1932.
A few trial proofs.
Run of 27 numbered and signed proofs
on different types of paper. Stone polished out.
1920. Drawing on paper transferred to stone.
Transfer effected by Pitault in 1932.
A few trial proofs.
Run of 26 numbered and signed proofs
on different types of paper. Stone polished out.

VII. THREE HORSES BY THE SEA

December 30th, 1920.
Format 6-1/2"x5" (16,5x12,5 cm).
Crayon drawing on lithograph paper
transferred to stone. 3 trial proofs.
Run of 3 proofs on Arches wove paper,
numbered and signed.
(Bruant, printer). Stone polished out.

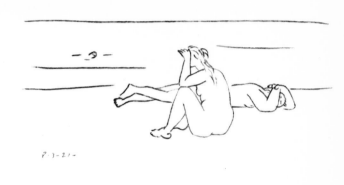

VIII. THE HORSEMAN. Format 7-3/4″x10-3/4″ (19,5x27 cm).

X. ON THE BEACH. 2 nudes. Format 4″x8-3/4″ (10x22 cm).

IX. THE WRESTLERS. Format 4-1/4″x7-3/4 (10,8x19,5 cm).

XI. ON THE BEACH. 3 nudes. Format 4-1/4″x7-1/2″ (11x19 cm).

VIII to XI. FOUR LITHOGRAPHS

1921. The four lithographs, made on stone,
were published by M. de Zayas and issued under a single printed cover.
Later the Galerie Simon bought the copies retained by the artist.
The Galerie Simon publishing sign was pasted on the cover
and the date altered, by hand, to 1928. A few trial proofs.
Run of 50 copies on Arches wove paper, signed and numbered.
Format of cover 14″x11-1/2″ (35x29 cm).
Format of paper, Nos VIII and X, 9″x11″ (23x28 cm)
Nos IX and XI, 8-3/4″x12-1/2″ (22,5x31,5 cm).
(Bruant, printer). Stones polished out.

XII. TWO WOMEN LYING AMONG THE SAND DUNES

XIII. THE FLORAL CROWN | XIV. COIFFURE | XV. LA TOILETTE

 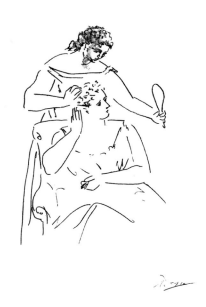 

XII. TWO WOMEN LYING AMONG THE SAND DUNES

1923. Format 8-3/4″ x 11-3/4″ (22 x 30 cm).
Crayon lithograph on stone.
2 trial proofs on Hollande Van Gelder paper
(Charlot Frères, printers). Stone polished out.

XIII. THE FLORAL CROWN

1923. Format 11-3/4″ x 9-1/4″ (29,7 x 23,8 cm).
Crayon drawing on stone. 4 trial proofs.
(Charlot Frères, printers). Stone polished out.

XIV. COIFFURE

1923. Format 10-1/4″ x 6-1/2″ (26,1 x 16,7 cm).
Lithographic crayon drawing on stone.
5 trial proofs.
Run of 50 proofs on Hollande Van Gelder paper,
signed and numbered.
Nos 1 to 25 on white wove paper,
Nos 26 to 50 on tinted wove paper.
Editions Galerie Simon (Charlot Frères, printers).
Stone polished out.

XV. LA TOILETTE

1923. Format 10-3/4″ x 8″ (27 x 20,4 cm).
Lithographic crayon drawing on stone.
5 trial proofs.
Run of 50 numbered and signed proofs
on Hollande Van Gelder paper.
Nos 1 to 25 on white wove paper,
Nos 26 to 50 on tinted wove paper.
Editions Galerie Simon (Charlot Frères, printers).
Stone polished out.

XVI. WOMAN WITH CHILD

XVII. WOMAN BY THE SEA

XVIII. RECLINING WOMAN

XIX. SEATED WOMAN

XVI. WOMAN WITH CHILD

1923. Format 7-3/4"x11-1/2" (19,5 x 29 cm).
Lithographic crayon drawing on stone.
5 trial proofs.
Run of 50 numbered and signed proofs
on Hollande Van Gelder paper.
Nos 1 to 25 on white wove paper,
Nos 26 to 50 on tinted wove paper.
Editions Galerie Simon (Charlot Frères, printers).
Stone polished out.

XVII. WOMAN BY THE SEA

1924. Format 8"x12" (20 x 30,8 cm).
Lithographic crayon drawing on stone. 5 trial proofs.
Run of 50 numbered and signed proofs on Hollande
Van Gelder paper. Nos 1 to 25 on white wove paper.
Nos 26 to 50 on tinted wove paper.
Editions Galerie Simon (Charlot Frères, printers).
Stone polished out.

XVIII. RECLINING WOMAN

1924. Format 8-1/2"x11-3" (21,6 x 30 cm).
Lithographic crayon drawing on stone. 5 trial proofs.

Run of 50 numbered and signed proofs on Hollande
Van Gelder paper. Nos 1 to 25 on white wove paper,
Nos 26 to 50 on tinted wove paper. Editions Galerie
Simon (Charlot Frères, printers). Stone polished out.

XIX. SEATED WOMAN

1924. Format 11-1/2"x8-1/4" (29,5 x 21 cm).
Crayon drawing on stone. 5 trial proofs.
Run of 50 numbered and signed proofs on Hollande
Van Gelder paper. Nos 1 to 25 on tinted wove paper.
Editions Galerie Simon (Charlot Frères, printers).
Stone polished out.

XX. WOMAN'S HEAD

XXI. INTERIOR SCENE

XXII. READING

XX. WOMAN'S HEAD

1925. Format 5" x 4-1/2" (12,7 x 11,5 cm).
Crayon drawing on stone; all the white sections
have been obtained by scraping as
in a wood engraving. Several artist's and trial proofs
on various types of paper. 100 numbered and signed
proofs on Japanese Imperial paper, inserted in the first
hundred copies of Waldemar George's book :
"Picasso, Dessins", ("Picasso, Drawings").
Editions des Quatre-Chemins, 1926,
format of book 11" x 9" (28 x 22,5 cm).
(Engelmann, printer). Stone polished out.

XXI. INTERIOR SCENE

1926. Format 8-3/4" x 11" (22,3 x 28 cm).
Crayon on stone composition. 5 trial proofs.
100 signed and numbered proofs on
Van Gelder paper.
Nos 1 to 50 on tinted wove paper,
Nos 51 to 100 on white wove paper.
Editions Galerie Simon (Charlot Frères, printers).
Stone polished out.

XXII. READING

1926. Format of the composition
and of the stone 13" x 9-1/2" (32,7 x 24,5 cm).
Crayon on stone. The child shows signs
of considerable scratching. 5 trial proofs.
Run of 100 signed and numbered proofs
on Van Gelder wove paper.
Nos 1 to 50 enriched with a buff
coloured background.
Nos 51 to 100 in black. Stone polished out.

XXIII. VISAGE

XXIV. HEAD OF YOUNG GIRL

3rd state

XXIII. VISAGE

1928. Format 8"5 x -3/4" (20,4 x 14,2 cm). Crayon on stone.
Trial proofs and 12 artist's proofs on various types of paper.
Run of 120 proofs on Japan paper for the de luxe copies
of André Level's book "Picasso". Publisher G. Grès, 1928.
Format of book 10-1/4" x 7-1/4" (26 x 18,5 cm).
A special run of 100 signed proofs was made of which 25 were
on mounted India paper and 75 on wide margin Japan paper.
Editions Galerie Percier (Marchizet, printer). Stone polished out.

XXIV. HEAD OF YOUNG GIRL

1928. Format 8-3/4" x 6-3/4" (22 x 17,2 cm).
Brush and crayon drawing on stone.
1st state. Reproduced.
2nd state. Scrapings in the background.
3rd state. Reproduced.
The traces in the background
have practically disappeared.
4th state. The background is entirely clear
and the face very lightly drawn.
11 proofs of each of these states (Duchâtel, printer)
Stone polished out.

XXV. FACE AND PROFILE

XXVII. THE PAINTER AND HIS MODEL

XXVI. FIGURE

XXV. FACE AND PROFILE

1928. Format 8-1/2" x 5" (21,8 x 12,4 cm).
Pen and wash drawing on stone.
The inking was not successful.
3 numbered and signed trial proofs.
Stone polished out.

XXVI. FIGURE

May 1929. Format 9-1/4" x 5-1/2" (23,7 x 13,8 cm).
Crayon on stone composition.
A few trial and artist's proofs.
Run of 300 proofs on Lafuma wove paper,
neither signed nor numbered, reserved for subscribers
to the magazine "Le Manuscrit Autographe"
(inset plate of No 21. May-June 1929).
Paper-book format 11" x 8-3/4" (28 x 22,5 cm)
Auguste Blaizot et fils, éditeurs.
Stone polished out.

XXVII. THE PAINTER AND HIS MODEL

1930. Format 9-1/4" x 11-1/2" (23,2 x 28,9 cm).
Crayon lithograph on stone.
10 trial proofs and 10 artist's proofs on various
types of paper. 50 signed and numbered proofs
on India paper mounted on Arches wove paper,
in addition to the copies on Arches wove paper,
Nos 1 to 50, for Eugenio d'Ors' book
"Pablo Picasso".
Editions des Chroniques du Jour, 1930,
format of the book 11" x 8-3/4" (28 x 22 cm).
(Desjobert, printer). Stone polished out.

On November 2nd 1945, Picasso came to work
at the printer's in Rue de Chabrol and scarcely left
the premises for four months.
He would come in a 9 o'clock in the morning
and work continuously until late at night,
often after 8 p.m. The artist tried out and utilized
all the different techniques: transfer paper,
stone, zinc, crayon, pen, wash drawing, etc.,
employing all the old methods of the craft.

All states of each lithograph are reproduced
hereafter; details below the reproductions indicate
the format of the proof paper.
Since almost all the prints were made
on thick Arches wove paper,
we felt it necessary to only mention the exceptions.
Finally, all the lithographs in signed
and numbered runs were published by
the Galerie Louise Leiris of Paris.
The format, mentioned in inches and centimetres,
refers to the lithograph itself
except where otherwise stated.

4. WOMAN'S HEAD

2. WOMAN'S HEAD ON BLACK
BACKGROUND

3. STYLIZED WOMAN'S HEAD
ON A BLACK BACKGROUND

1st state

1. WOMAN'S HEAD

1. WOMAN'S HEAD

November 2nd, 1945.
Format of lithograph
13-1/2" x 10-1/4" (34 x 26 cm).
Ink covered lithographic paper cut out and pasted,
then transferred to stone.
18 artist reserved proofs.
50 numbered and signed proofs.
Stone polished out.

2. WOMAN'S HEAD ON BLACK BACKGROUND

November 2nd, 1945.
Format of lithograph 12" x 9" (30,5 x 23 cm).
Solid lithographic ink on lithographic paper
transferred to stone, the white line was achieved
by scraping off with a knife on the paper.
18 artist reserved proofs.
50 numbered and signed proofs.
Stone polished out.

3. STYLIZED WOMAN'S HEAD ON A BLACK
BACKGROUND

November 2nd, 1945.
Format of lithograph 12-1/4" x 9" (31 x 23 cm).
Same process as for stone No 2.
18 artist reserved proofs.
50 numbered and signed proofs.
Stone polished out.

1st state

2nd state

5. HEAD OF YOUNG GIRL

3rd state

4th state

2nd state

4. WOMAN'S HEAD

1st state. November 2nd, 1945.
Format of lithograph 12-1/4" x 9-1/2" (31 x 24 cm).
Lithographic paper worked on with crayon
and transferred to stone. 18 artist reserved proofs.
2nd state. December 20th, 1945.
The stone was scraped in various places;
the date remains November 2nd, 1945.
18 artist's proofs. Stone polished out.

5. HEAD OF YOUNG GIRL

1st state. November 5th, 1945.
Format of drawing 9-1/2" x 6-1/2" (24 x 16,5 cm).
Crayon and pen on lithographic paper
transferred to stone.   18 artist reserved proofs.
2nd state. November 24th, 1945.
The drawing has been re-worked by pen, scrapings.
18 artist reserved proofs.
3rd state. November 26th, 1945.
Wash drawing; scrapings.
18 artist reserved proofs.

4th state. December 17th, 1945.
Format of drawing 10-3/4" x 8-1/4" (27 x 21 cm).
Scrapings. 18 artist's proofs.
50 numbered and signed proofs.
Stone polished out.

6. STILL LIFE WITH FRUIT STAND

1st state

3rd state

2nd state

14

6. STILL LIFE WITH FRUIT STAND

1st state. November 6th, 1945.
Format 13-1/2" x 9-1/2" (34,5 x 24,5 cm). Work executed
on stone with crayon, ink and drỹ brush. 3 trial proofs.
2nd state. November 12th, 1945.
Re-worked with ink: scrapings. 18 artist reserved proofs.
3rd state. November 16th, 1945.
Format 14" x 9-3/4" (35,5 x 24,5 cm).
Crayon in the background, scraping in the foreground.
18 artist reserved proofs.
50 signed and numbered proofs. Stone polished out.

| 7. HEAD OF YOUNG GIRL | *1st state* | *2nd state* | *3rd state* |

| 8. HEAD OF YOUNG BOY | *1st state* | *2nd state* | *3rd state* |

7. HEAD OF YOUNG GIRL

1st state. November 5th, 1945.
Format of the lithograph
11-3/4" x 8-3/4" (30 x 22 cm).
Ink drawing executed on lithographic paper
with scrapings and transferred to stone.
18 artist reserved proofs.
2nd state. November 25th, 1945.
The face has been entirely re-worked
with a small paint brush. 18 artist reserved proofs.
3rd state. December 2nd, 1945.
The face has been cleared with a scraper.

On the stone, the date remains
November 5th, 1945
Only 18 artist reserved proofs were printed
of the 3rd state, the stone having been
polished out in error.

8. HEAD OF YOUNG BOY

1st state. November 7th, 1945.
Format of the background
11-1/2" x 9" (29 x 23 cm).
Ink drawing with scrapings on lithographic paper
transferred to stone. 18 artist reserved proofs.

2nd state. November 7th, 1945.
Wash drawing added in the face. 2 trial proofs.
3rd state. The stone was immediately re-worked.
Shading accentuated in the face, and scrapings.
The date remains November 7th, 1945.
18 artist reserved proofs.
50 signed and numbered proofs.
Stone polished out.

1st state

2nd state

3rd state

6th state

7th state

9. HEAD OF YOUNG GIRL

16

9. HEAD OF YOUNG GIRL

1st state. November 7th, 1945.
Format of stone 12-3/4" x 10-1/4" (32 x 26 cm).
Wash drawing on stone.
2nd state. November 9th, 1945.
The composition has been completely changed.
The whole surface of the stone has been ink covered.
The place occupied by a small splinter at the top of
the stone is still visible in the subsequent states.
Brush drawing and scrapings.
3rd state. November 12th, 1945.
Wash drawing and scrapings.

4th state. November 15th, 1945.
Wash drawing continuous tone; scraper.
5th state. November 22nd, 1945.
The face is scraped and re-worked in crayon.
6th state. November 26th, 1945.
Shadings accentuated with lithographic crayon,
background darkened.
7th state. December 2nd, 1945.
Scrapings with the flat of a blade
and with a scraper.

4th state

5th state

8th state

9th state

10th state

8th state. January 17th, 1946.
The drawing has changed, brush and scraper.
9th state. February 6th, 1946.
Brush, scrapings.
10th state. February 19th, 1946.
Only slight alterations, pen and scrapings.
The following proofs were made of this lithograph:
1st state: 2 trial proofs.
2nd to 9th state: 18 artist reserved proofs.
10th state: 18 artist reserved proofs,
50 signed and numbered proofs.

10. TWO SMALL BULLS

11. BULLFIGHT SCENES

10. TWO SMALL BULLS

December 15th, 1945.
Format of the composition
10-1/4" x 5-1/2" (26 x 14 cm).
Scraped lithographic ink solid plate,
cut out and pasted on lithographic paper
and transferred to stone.
18 artist reserved proofs.
Stone polished out.

11. BULLFIGHT SCENES

December 15th, 1945.
Format 15-3/4" x 23-3/4" (40 x 60 cm).
Same working method as for the preceding lithograph.
A single proof on ordinary paper.
Stone polished out.

1st state   *2nd state*   *3rd state*

12. LONG-HAIRED YOUNG GIRL

4th state   *5th state*   *6th state*

19

12. LONG-HAIRED YOUNG GIRL

1st state. November 6th, 1945.
Format 15" x 12-1/2" (38 x 32 cm).
Lithograph on stone with soft crayon. 2 trial proofs.
2nd state. November 7th, 1945.
Scrapings and detail changes with crayon;
an eye and the mouth, insufficiently scraped,
come out on the proof.
3rd state. November 9th, 1945.
Crayon. Scrapings.
4th state. November 16th, 1945.
Carrying on of this work in the following states.

5th state. November 20th 1945.
6th state. November 24th, 1945.
The line is strengthened and the background
completely scraped. 18 artist's proofs
were made from each of these six states
with the exception of the first.
50 signed and numbered proofs
made of the 6th state.
Stone polished out.

13. COMPOSITION

20

13. COMPOSITION

This two-tone lithograph, as well as two subsequent ones,
were produced when Picasso was trying to find
a suitable expression medium
for the illustration of Reverdy's manuscript "Le Chant des Morts"
Tériade, publisher. November 10th, 1945.
Format 16" x 12" (41 x 30 cm).
Bistre : one coating after a wash drawing on lithographic paper
transferred to stone, a second coating
of the same tone, wash drawing on stone.
Black : lithographic crayon drawing on paper transferred to stone.
A single trial proof on ordinary paper.

14. COMPOSITION

15. ARABESQUE

14. COMPOSITION

November 11th, 1945. Format 13" x 9" (33 x 23 cm).
The red and the black executed in crayon and wash drawing
on lithographic paper transferred to stone.
A single trial proof.

15. ARABESQUE

November 12th, 1945. Wash drawing on stone.
As we shall see later, the artist chose
this process to illustrate "Le Chant des Morts".
18 proofs made in red. Stone polished out.

16. TWO NUDE WOMEN

1st state

2nd state

3rd state

4th state

16. TWO NUDE WOMEN

1st state. November 10th 1945.
Format of the composition 10" x 13" (25 x 33 cm).
Wash drawing on stone.
2nd state. November 13th, 1945.
The drawing has been strengthened
by wash drawing.
3rd state. November 21st, 1945.
Drawing more elaborated by pen; scrapings.
4th state. November 22nd, 1945.
Work with pen and scraper continued.

5th state

6th state

7th state

8th state

23

5th state. November 24th, 1945.
Addition of pure blacks with a brush, scrapings.
At this point the artist made a special stone
with crayon for a second colour.
Two proofs were made in bistre but proved
unsatisfactory and the stone was polished out.
6th state. November 26th, 1945.
Appearance of a screen on the left of the composition
note the fine pen work in the reclining figure.

7th state. December 30th, 1945.
The beginning of a transformation in the drawing;
wash drawing in the margins.
Picasso painted a few aquarelles,
with the lithographic composition in mind,
at his own home and the following day had proofs
made from the stone on to these aquarelles.
6 proofs, coloured before pressing,
exist of this lithograph.
8th state. January 5th, 1946.
Numerous erasures and scrapings.

16. TWO NUDE WOMEN

9th state

10th state

11th state

12th state

9th state. January 10th, 1946.
The drawing has changed; pen, wash drawing
and scrapings. The margin is cleaned.
10th state. January 17th, 1946.
From this state onwards, the composition changed
Each time the artist returned to his stone.
Wash drawing, pen and scrapings.
11th state. January 21st, 1946.
12th state. January 24th, 1946.

13th state

14th state

15th state

16th state

13th state. January 25th, 1946.
14th state. January 31st, 1946.
15th state. February 1st, 1946.
The surface of the stone, which had been scraped
very many times, at this point
appeared full of hollows and reliefs;
this state was pressed on a fairly soft paper
which retained in relief the hollows of the stone.
16th state. February 6th, 1946.
The composition has taken on a new aspect,
black in the background and with three small profiles
in the left hand margin.

17th state

18th state

17th state. February 8th, 1946.
Changes, cleaning of the margin.
18th state. February 12th, 1946.
Final change in the composition;
drawings in the margins, birds and large insects.

19 trial proofs reserved for the artist
were made from each of these 18 states.
50 signed and numbered proofs were also made of
the final state. Stone polished out.
Proof in black of the second stone
made for the 5th state.

Here the 2nd stone has been pressed in bistre
on a proof of the 5th state.
The result was unsatisfactory
and the artist had it destroyed immediately.
2 proofs on ordinary paper.

17. THE BULL

1st state

2nd state

17. THE BULL

1st state. December 5th, 1945.
Format of drawing 11-1/2" x 16-1/2" (29 x 42 cm).
Wash drawing on stone.
2nd state. December 12th, 1945.
The previous wash drawing is completely
re-worked and re-drawn in wash drawing and pen.

3rd state

4th state

6th state

17. THE BULL

3rd state. December 18th, 1945.
Scraping with the flat of the blade followed
by very elaborate pen work.
4th state. December 22nd, 1945.
Pen and scrapings.
5th state. December 24th, 1945.
Each time the artist returned to the stone
he simplified his drawing using pen and scraper.
6th state. December 26th, 1945.
7th state. December 28th, 1945.
8th state. January 2nd, 1946.

17. THE BULL

5th state

7th state

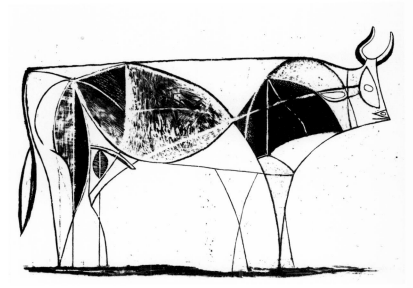

8th state

29

17. THE BULL

9th state

10th state   *11th state*

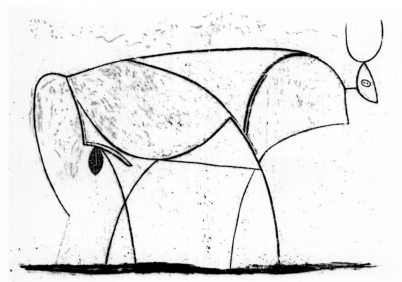

30

9th state. January 5th, 1946.
10th state. January 10th, 1946.
11th state. January 17th, 1946.
The drawing has been reduced to its simplest form;
only a few traces of wash drawing and crayon
remain on the stone. Format of the subject
11-1/2″×10-3/4″ (29×27,5 cm).

18 artist reserved proofs were made of each
of the 11 states of this lithograph. In addition
50 signed and numbered proofs were made
of the 11th state. Stone polished out.

18. PAGE OF SKETCHES

19. HEADS OF RAMS

18. PAGE OF SKETCHES
(Heads of children and horses)

December 4th, 1945.
Format of the composition
15-3/4"x10-3/4" (40x27 cm).
Drawings made on stone with pen and
wash drawing; scrapings.
18 artist reserved proofs.
50 signed and numbered proofs.
Stone polished out.

19. HEADS OF RAMS

December 7th, 1945.
Format of the composition
13-1/2"x9" (34x23 cm).
Wash drawing and pen drawings on stone.
18 artist reserved proofs.
50 signed and numbered proofs.
Stone polished out.

20. STILL LIFE WITH VASE OF FLOWERS

21. BULLS, RAMS AND BIRDS

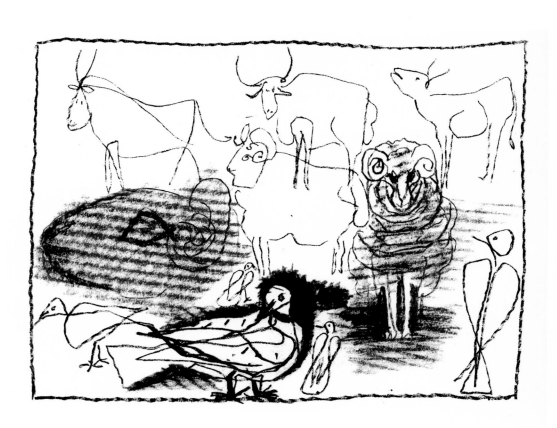

20. STILL LIFE WITH VASE OF FLOWERS

December 14th, 1945.
Format 17-1/2" x 12-3/4" (44 x 32,5 cm).
Wash drawing on stone.
The central part came out too faint.
A single proof on ordinary paper.
Stone polished out immediately.

21. BULLS, RAMS AND BIRDS

December 22nd, 1945.
Format 15-3/4" x 11-3/4" (40 x 30 cm).
Page of lithographic crayon drawings
on transfer paper placed, as
with the two following items, on corrugated paper.
18 artist's proofs. Stone polished out.

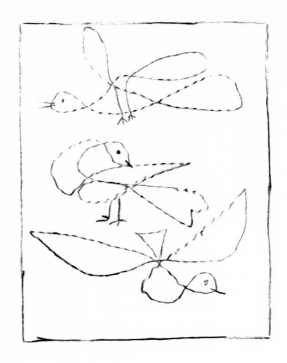

23. BIRDS IN FLIGHT

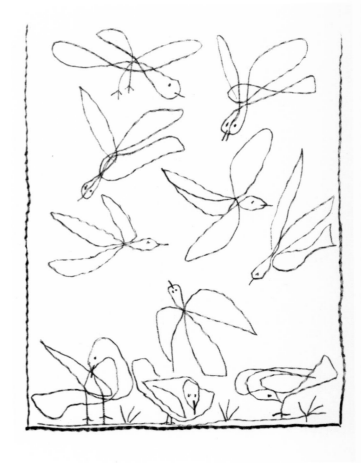

22. THREE BIRDS

22. THREE BIRDS

December 22nd, 1945.
Format 12-3/4" x 9-1/2" (32 x 24 cm).
Soft lithographic crayon on paper
transferred to stone. 18 artist reserved proofs.
Stone polished out.

23. BIRDS IN FLIGHT

December 22nd, 1945.
Format 16-1/4 x 12-1/4" (41 x 31 cm).
Lithographic crayon on paper transferred to stone.
18 artist reserved proofs. Stone polished out.

24. THE CIRCUS

1st state

2nd state

34

24. THE CIRCUS

1st state. December 20th, 1945.
Format 15-1/2" x 11-1/2" (39 x 29 cm).
Lithographic paper worked in ink,
cut out and pasted, then transferred to stone.
18 artist reserved proofs.
2nd state. December 23rd, 1945.
The horse and the spectators re-touched with ink.
Faces scraped on the right of the drawing.
18 artist reserved proofs.
50 signed and numbered proofs. Stone polished out.

25. BULLFIGHT UNDER A BLACK SUN

25. BULLFIGHT UNDER A BLACK SUN

January 7th, 1946.
Format 16-1/4" x 11-3/4" (41 x 30 cm).
Lithographic paper worked in rubbed crayon
and ink, cut out and pasted, then transferred to stone.
18 artist reserved proofs.
Stone polished out

26. BULLFIGHT

26. BULLFIGHT

January 7th, 1946.
Format 16″x11-3/4″ (43x29,5 cm).
Same method of working as in the previous item.
18 artist reserved proofs.
50 signed and numbered proofs.
Stone polished out.

27. SIDE VIEW OF BULL

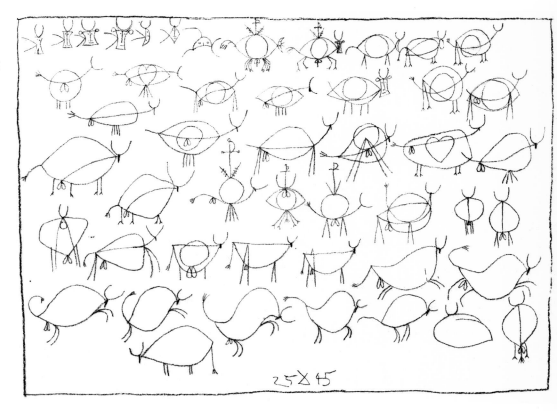

28. PAGE OF BULLS

27. SIDE VIEW OF BULL

December 25th, 1945.
Format 16-1/2″ x 11-1/2″ (42 x 29 cm).
Crayon lithograph on paper transferred to stone.
18 artist reserved proofs.
Stone polished out.

28. PAGE OF BULLS

December 25th, 1945.
Format 17″ x 12-1/4″ (43 x 31 cm).
Numerous drawings of bulls in crayon
on litho paper and transferred to stone.
18 artist reserved proofs. Stone polished out.

29. EIGHT SILHOUETTES

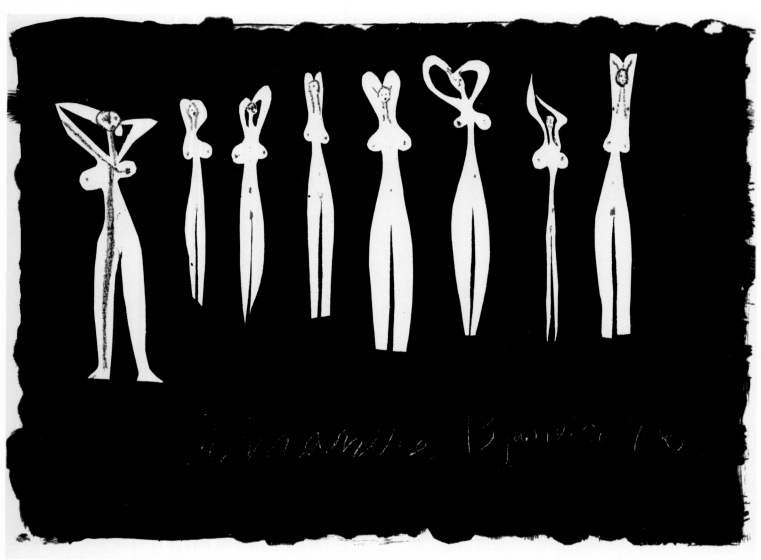

29. EIGHT SILHOUETTES

January 13th, 1946.
Format 17" x 12-1/2" (43 x 32 cm).
Papers cut out, worked in crayon and pasted
on flat tint lithographic ink paper,
text scratched out, then transferred to stone.
18 artist reserved proofs.
50 signed and numbered proofs.
Stone polished out.

30. STILL LIFE WITH
THREE APPLES

31. STILL LIFE WITH
THREE APPLES

30. STILL LIFE WITH THREE APPLES

December 15th, 1945.
Format 14-1/4" x 9-3/4" (36 x 25 cm).
Lithograph in 4 colours, plus black.
The coloured stones were executed from a flat tint
ink paper following reproduction proofs.
The black stone was executed with crayon.
18 artist reserved proofs.
Black stone polished out.

31. STILL LIFE WITH THREE APPLES

December 17th, 1945.
Format 14-1/4" x 9-3/4" (36 x 25 cm).
Variation on the previous composition.
Only three basic colours were pressed;
the black was made in wash drawing on
lithographic paper
cut out and transferred to stone.
2 proofs of the black; 1 colour proof.
Stones polished out.

1st state

32. COMPOSITION

2nd state

3rd state

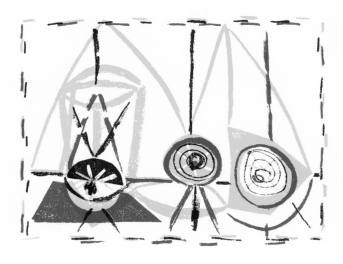

40

32. COMPOSITION

1st state. January 13th, 1946.
Format 12-1/2" x 9-1/2" (32 x 24 cm).
Lithograph in three colours.
Each colour prepared in crayon
on pasted paper and transferred to stone.
2nd state. February 8th, 1946.
Each stone re-worked in crayon and with scraper.

3rd state. February 18th, 1946.
The composition has been reinforced with crayon.
18 artist reserved proofs of each state.
50 proofs were made of this lithograph
on Japan Hodomura paper.
It was used for the set of prints included
with the first fifty copies of the book
"Dans l'Atelier de Picasso" ("In Picasso's studio"),
Fernand Mourlot, publisher.

33. COMPOSITION WITH GLASS AND APPLE

3rd state

33. COMPOSITION WITH GLASS AND APPLE

1st state. January 13th, 1946.
Format 12-1/2" x 9-1/2" (32 x 24 cm).
Lithograph in three colours.
Each colour effected in crayon.
2nd state. February 7th, 1946.
Crayon added to each stone.

3rd state. February 18th, 1946.
Format of drawing 13-3/4" x 11" (35 x 28 cm).
Composition re-worked in all three colours.
18 artist reserved proofs of each state.
50 proofs of this lithograph were made
on Japan Hodomura paper.
It was used for the set of prints included
with the first fifty copies of the book
"Dans l'Atelier de Picasso" ("In Picasso's studio"),
Fernand Mourlot, publisher.

2nd state

34. SHELLS AND BIRDS

34. SHELLS AND BIRDS

1st state. February 14th, 1946.
Format 13″ x 9″ (33 x 23 cm).
Wash drawing and pen on stone.
18 artist reserved proofs.
2nd state. February 19th, 1946.
The stone is re-worked: wash drawing and pen.
18 artist reserved proofs.
50 signed and numbered proofs.
Stone polished out.

35. THE BLACK PITCHER AND THE DEATH'S HEAD

36. COMPOSITION WITH SKULL

43

35. THE BLACK PITCHER AND THE DEATH'S HEAD

February 20th, 1946.
Format 12-3/4" x 17-1/2" (32,5 x 44 cm).
Crayon and ink composition on lithographic paper
transferred to stone; scrapings.
18 artist reserved proofs.
50 signed and numbered proofs.
Stone polished out.

36. COMPOSITION WITH SKULL

February 20th, 1946.
Format 20" x 25-1/2" (50 x 65 cm).
Crayon composition on lithographic paper,
transferred to stone. 6 artist reserved proofs
pressed in the 22" x 30" format (56 x 76 cm)
on Vidalon wove paper.
Stone polished out.

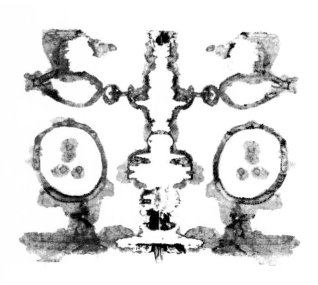

37. STUDIES

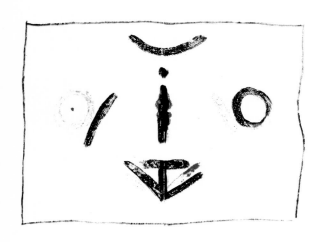

37. STUDIES

February 21st, 1946.
Formats 11-1/2″×9-1/2″ (29×24 cm).
and 7-1/2″×6-3/4″ (19×17 cm).
Trials of lithographic materials using
wash drawing, crayon and scraper
on lithographic paper transferred to stone.
2 proofs of each of the five stones.
Stones polished out.

38. FRANÇOISE

39. FRANÇOISE

45

38. FRANÇOISE

June 14th, 1946.
Format of drawing 23-1/4″ x 17″ (59 x 43 cm).
Crayon on lithographic paper transferred to stone.
3 trial proofs. Stone polished out.

39. FRANÇOISE

June 14th, 1946.
Format 21-1/4″ x 19″ (54 x 48 cm).
Crayon on lithographic paper transferred to stone.
3 trial proofs. Stone polished out.

40. FRANÇOISE

41. FRANÇOISE WITH A BOW IN HER HAIR

40. FRANÇOISE

June 14th, 1946.
Format 23-3/4" x 19-1/4" (60 x 49 cm).
Crayon on lithographic paper transferred to stone.
5 artist reserved proofs.
50 signed and numbered proofs.
Stone polished out.

41. FRANÇOISE WITH A BOW IN HER HAIR

June 14th, 1946.
Format 25" x 18-1/2" (63 x 47 cm).
Crayon drawing on lithographic paper
transferred to stone.
5 artist reserved proofs.
50 signed and numbered proofs.
Stone polished out.

42. FRANÇOISE

43. FRANÇOISE

44. FRANÇOISE

42. FRANÇOISE

June 14th, 1946. Format 25"x18-1/2" (63x47 cm).
Crayon on lithographic paper transferred to stone.
5 artist reserved proofs.
50 signed and numbered proofs. Stone polished out.

43. FRANÇOISE

June 14th, 1946. Format 25"x18-1/2" (63x47 cm).
Crayon on lithographic paper transferred to stone.
5 artist reserved proofs.
50 signed and numbered proofs. Stone polished out.

44. FRANÇOISE

June 14th, 1946.
Format 25"x19-1/4" (63x49 cm).
Crayon on lithographic paper transferred to stone.
5 artist reserved proofs.
50 signed and numbered proofs.
Stone polished out.

45. FRANÇOISE

46. FRANÇOISE

48

45. FRANÇOISE

June 14th, 1946.
Format 25"x19" (63x48 cm).
Crayon on lithographic paper transferred to stone.
5 artist reserved proofs.
50 signed and numbered proofs.
Stone polished out.

46. FRANÇOISE

June 14th, 1946.
Format 24"x18" (61x46 cm).
Crayon on lithographic paper transferred to stone.
5 artist reserved proofs.
50 signed and numbered proofs.
Stone polished out.

14 juin 46

47. FRANÇOISE WITH WAVY HAIR

48. FRANÇOISE THE SUN WOMAN

47. FRANÇOISE WITH WAVY HAIR

June 14th, 1946.
Format 25"x19" (63x48 cm).
Crayon on lithographic paper transferred
to stone; scrapings.
5 artist reserved proofs.
50 signed and numbered proofs.
Stone polished out.

48. FRANÇOISE THE SUN WOMAN

June 15th, 1946.
Format 21"x17-3/4" (53x45 cm).
Rubbed crayon drawing on lithographic paper,
then papers cut and pasted,
and transferred to stone.
5 artist reserved proofs.
50 signed and numbered proofs.
Stone polished out.

49. TWO TURTLE-DOVES I

50. TWO TURTLE-DOVES II

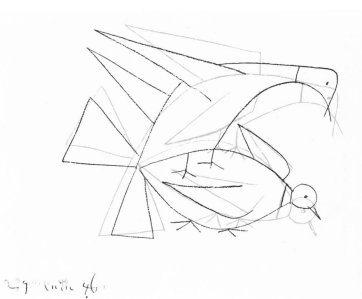

51. THE TWO TURTLE-DOVES, DOUBLE IMAGE

49. TWO TURTLE-DOVES I

June 29th, 1946.
Format 17"x12-3/4" (43x32 cm).
Crayon on lithographic paper transferred to stone.
Stamped in purple-red.
5 artist reserved proofs.
25 signed and numbered proofs.

50. TWO TURTLE-DOVES II

June 29th, 1946.
Format 17-1/2"x13-3/4" (44x35 cm).
Variation on the preceding composition. Stamped
in yellow-gold. 5 artist reserved proofs.
25 signed and numbered proofs.

51. THE TWO TURTLE-DOVES, DOUBLE IMAGE

The violet and yellow lithographs superimposed.
5 artist reserved proofs.
25 signed and numbered proofs. Stones polished out

52. HEAD OF A YOUNG WOMAN

53. OWL WITH WHITE BACKGROUND

52. HEAD OF A YOUNG WOMAN

July 3rd, 1946.
Format 12" x 8-1/2" (30 x 21,5 cm).
Signed and dated crayon drawing
on lithographic paper transferred to stone.
6 trial proofs. Stone retained and stored.

53. OWL WITH WHITE BACKGROUND

January 20th, 1947.
Format 25-1/2" x 16-1/2" (64 x 42 cm).
Wash drawing and rubbed crayon composition;
scrapings. Transferred to stone.
5 artist reserved proofs.
50 signed and numbered proofs.
Stone polished out.

54. OWL WITH CHAIR

55. OWL WITH CHAIR, OCHRE BACKGROUND

54. OWL WITH CHAIR

January 20th, 1947.
Format 25-1/2" x 19-3/4" (64 x 50 cm).
Wash drawing and rubbed crayon composition,
scrapings can be seen in the bird.
Transferred to stone.
5 artist reserved proofs.
25 signed and numbered proofs.

55. OWL WITH CHAIR, OCHRE BACKGROUND

January 20th, 1947.
Format 25-1/2" x 19-3/4" (64 x 50 cm).
The artist produced a stone, using rubbed crayon,
to give a colour background
for the preceding composition.
It was stamped in yellow ochre.
5 artist reserved proofs.
25 signed and numbered proofs.
Stones polished out.

56. THE BLACK OWL

56. THE BLACK OWL

January 21st, 1947.
Format 25" x 19" (63 x 48 cm).
Crayon and wash drawing composition;
transferred to stone.
5 artist reserved proofs.
50 signed and numbered proofs.
Stone polished out.

57. OWL IN CRAYON

January 21st, 1947.
Format 25-1/2" x 19" (64 x 48 cm).
Crayon composition on lithographic paper;
transferred to stone.
5 artist reserved proofs.
50 signed and numbered proofs.
Stone polished out.

58. CENTAURS PLAYING

59. FAUNS AND THE SHE-CENTAUR

54

58. CENTAURS PLAYING

January 27th, 1947.
Format 15-3/4" x 21-1/4" (40 x 54 cm).
Pen and rubbed crayon drawing
on lithographic paper; transferred to stone.
This composition has been badly transferred.
In fact, it can be seen that the left
hand part of the drawing is clear, whereas
two-thirds of the sheet has stretched producing
on the right a double impression of the lines.
One single proof. Stone polished out.

59. FAUNS AND THE SHE-CENTAUR

January 26th, 1947.
Format 19-1/4" x 25-1/2" (49 x 64 cm).
Pen and crayon composition on lithographic paper;
transferred to stone.
5 artist reserved proofs.
50 signed and numbered proofs.
Stone polished out.

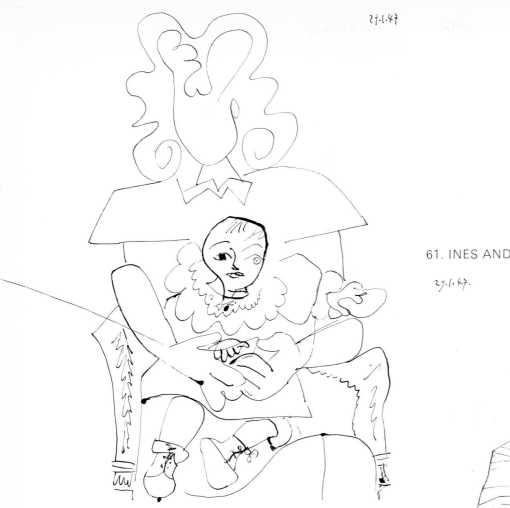

60. INES AND HER CHILD

61. INES AND HER CHILD

60. INES AND HER CHILD

January 29th, 1947.
Format 25"x15-1/4" (63x39 cm).
Pen drawing on lithographic paper
transferred to stone.
5 artist reserved proofs.
50 signed and numbered proofs.
Stone polished out.

61. INES AND HER CHILD

January 29th, 1947.
Format 25-1/4"x18-1/2" (64x47 cm).
Pen drawing on lithographic paper
with some crayon rubbing, transferred to stone.
5 artist reserved proofs.
50 signed and numbered proofs.
Stone polished out.

62. CENTAUR AND BACCHANTE

62. CENTAUR AND BACCHANTE

February 2nd, 1947.
Format 21-1/4"x19" (54x48 cm).
Wash drawing and pen composition
on lithographic paper transferred to stone.
5 artist reserved proofs.
50 signed and numbered proofs.
Stone polished out.

63. CENTAUR AND BACCHANTE WITH FAUN

63. CENTAUR AND BACCHANTE WITH FAUN

February 2nd, 1947.
Format 25-1/4 x 19-1/4" (64 x 49 cm).
Wash drawing and rubbed crayon composition
with scrapings,
on lithographic paper transferred to stone.
5 artist reserved proofs.
50 signed and numbered proofs.
Stone polished out.

64. PIGEON ON GREY BACKGROUND

66. THE FAT PIGEON

65. WHITE PIGEON ON BLACK BACKGROUND

67. BUST OF A YOUNG GIRL

64. PIGEON ON GREY BACKGROUND

February 2nd, 1947. Format 17-3/4" x 10-3/4" (45 x 27 cm).
Gouache worked wash drawing on lithographic paper transferred
to stone. Unusual process utilized by the artist for the first time:
remarkable result. 5 artist reserved proofs.
50 signed and numbered proofs. Stone polished out.

65. WHITE PIGEON ON BLACK BACKGROUND

February 4th, 1947. Format 19" x 12-1/4" (48 x 31 cm).
Similar process to that of No. 64, flat tint; scrapings can be seen
in the ground. 5 artist reserved proofs.
50 signed and numbered proofs. Stone polished out.

66. THE FAT PIGEON

February 2nd, 1947. Format 20" x 15-3/4" (51 x 40 cm).
Wash drawing on lithographic paper transferred to stone.
5 artist reserved proofs. 50 signed and numbered proofs.
Stone polished out.

67. BUST OF A YOUNG GIRL

February 4th, 1947. Format 21-3/4" x 15-3/4" (55 x 40 cm).
Brush drawing on lithographic paper transferred to stone.
5 artist reserved proofs. 50 signed and numbered proofs.
Stone polished out.

68. HEAD OF A YOUNG GIRL

1st state

2nd state

68. HEAD OF A YOUNG GIRL

1st state. March 5th, 1947.
Format of the composition 17-3/4" x 14-1/2" (45 x 37 cm).
Wash drawing on zinc and pen lines. 2 trial proofs.
2nd state. March 10th, 1947.
Shadows reinforced with wash drawing.
5 artist reserved proofs.

3rd state

68. HEAD OF A YOUNG GIRL

4th state

60

68. HEAD OF A YOUNG GIRL

3rd state. The whole face is re-painted
in wash drawing; scrapings with blade and scraper.
5 artist reserved proofs.
4th state. Format 19-3/4" x 15-3/4" (50 x 40 cm).
The zinc is inked to the edges.
More wash drawing and scrapings.
5 artist reserved proofs.
50 signed and numbered proofs.
Zinc polished out.

69. WOMAN IN THE ARMCHAIR

69. WOMAN IN THE ARMCHAIR

February 16th, 1947. Format 12-3/4" x 18-1/2" (32 x 47 cm).
6 colour composition, yellow, red, green, blue, violet and black.
Each colour produced with crayon and ink on lithographic paper
and transferred to stone. 5 artist reserved proofs.
50 signed and numbered proofs. Stones polished out.

70. PORTRAIT OF GONGORA

71. YOUNG PIGEON IN ITS NEST

70. PORTRAIT OF GONGORA

March 5th, 1947.
Format 15-1/4" x 12-3/4" (39 x 32 cm).
Pen and wash drawing on zinc.
5 artist reserved proofs.
50 signed and numbered proofs.
Zinc polished out.

71. YOUNG PIGEON IN ITS NEST

March 11th, 1947. Format 15-1/2" x 8-1/2" (39,5 x 21,5 cm).
Wash drawing composition, use of scraper,
on lithographic paper transferred to stone.
5 artist reserved proofs. 50 signed and numbered proofs.
Stone polished out.

72. PIGEON AND ITS LITTLE ONES

73. LARGE STILL LIFE WITH FRUIT DISH

72. PIGEON AND ITS LITTLE ONES

March 19th, 1947.
Format 20-3/4" x 15-3/4" (53 x 40 cm).
Pen and brush composition on zinc.
5 artist reserved proofs.
50 signed and numbered proofs.
Zinc polished out.

73. LARGE STILL LIFE WITH FRUIT DISH

1st state. March 7th, 1947.
Format 24" x 18-1/2" (61 x 47 cm).
Wash drawing composition on zinc.
1 trial proof only.
2nd state. March 10th, 1947. Reproduced.
Reinforcing of the composition with wash drawing.
5 artist reserved proofs.
50 signed and numbered proofs.
Zinc polished out.

74. COMPOSITION
WITH VASE OF FLOWERS

75. COMPOSITION IN THREE COLOURS

74. COMPOSITION WITH VASE OF FLOWERS

March 10th, 1947.
Format 23-1/2" x 17-3/4" (60 x 45 cm).
Still life in three colours, grey, red-brown and black.
Composition made as follows: black by pen on zinc;
red with cut out lithographic paper pasted
and transferred to stone,
and grey by filling a reproduction proof on stone.
5 trial proofs retained by the artist.
50 signed and numbered proofs.
Zinc and stones polished out.

75. COMPOSITION IN THREE COLOURS

March 11th, 1947. Format 8" x 11" (20 x 28 cm).
Inked lithographic paper cut out and pasted.
Transferred to stone.
4 trial proofs. This lithograph appeared in the book
"Dans l'Atelier de Picasso" ("In Picasso's studio"),
Fernand Mourlot, publisher.
Run of 250 proofs on Arches wove paper.
50 proofs on Japan Hodomura paper,
for the set allotted to the first 50 copies.

78. THE KNIFE AND THE APPLE

76. APPLES, GLASS AND KNIFE

March 11th, 1947. Format 10-3/4" x 4" (27 x 10 cm).
Still life in wash drawing and pen on lithographic paper transferred to stone.
4 trial proofs. This lithograph appeared in the book
"Dans l'Atelier de Picasso" ("In Picasso's studio"), Fernand Mourlot, publisher.
Run of 250 proofs on Arches wove paper. 50 proofs on Japan Hodomura paper
destined for the set reserved for the first 50 copies.

77. COMPOSITION WITH STEMMED GLASS

79. THE SMALL BUNCH OF GRAPES

March 14th, 1947. Format 7-3/4" x 1-3/4" (20 x 4,5 cm).
Pen and wash drawing on lithographic paper transferred to stone.
4 trial proofs. This lithograph appeared in the book
"Dans l'Atelier de Picasso" ("In Picasso's studio"), Fernand Mourlot, publisher.
250 proofs on Arches wove paper. 50 proofs on Japan Hodomura paper
destined for the set reserved for the first 50 copies.

76. APPLES, GLASS AND KNIFE

March 11th, 1947. Format 11" x 6-3/4" (28 x 17 cm).
Ink and wash drawing composition on lithographic paper
transferred to stone. 4 trial proofs.
This lithograph, of which 50 proofs were made on Japan Hodomura paper,
was utilized for the set allotted to the first 50 copies of the book
"Dans l'Atelier de Picasso" ("In Picasso's studio"),
Fernand Mourlot, publisher.

77. COMPOSITION WITH STEMMED GLASS

March 12th, 1947. Format 12-1/4" x 10" (31 x 25 cm). Inked paper, cut out
and pasted, then work with pen on lithographic paper transferred to stone.
This lithograph, of which 50 proofs were made on Japan Hodomura paper,
was utilized for the set allotted to the first 50 copies of the book
"Dans l'Atelier de Picasso" ("In Picasso's studio"),
Fernand Mourlot, publisher.

80. COUPLE

82. PROFILE OF WOMAN

81. THE SLEEPING WOMAN

83. PROFILE ON BLACK BACKGROUND

80. COUPLE

March 23rd, 1947. Format 19-3/4" x 25-3/4" (50 x 65 cm).
Pen drawing on zinc.
5 artist reserved proofs. 50 signed and numbered proofs. Zinc polished out.

81. THE SLEEPING WOMAN

March 23rd, 1947. Format 19-3/4" x 25-3/4" (50 x 65 cm).
Pen and wash drawing composition on zinc.
5 artist proofs. 50 signed and numbered proofs. Zinc polished out.

82. PROFILE OF WOMAN

March 26th, .1947.
Format 19-3/4" x 13-1/2" (50 x 34 cm).
Pen drawing on zinc. 5 artist reserved proofs.
50 signed and numbered proofs. Zinc polished out.

83. PROFILE ON BLACK BACKGROUND

March 29th, 1947.
Format 20-3/4" x 14-1/4" (53 x 36 cm).
Drawing sketched out in crayon and executed in pen
and wash drawing on zinc. 5 artist reserved proofs.
50 signed and numbered proofs. Zinc polished out.

84. WOMAN WITH A NECKLACE

85. LARGE PROFILE

84. WOMAN WITH A NECKLACE

March 29th, 1947.
Format 24-1/2″x16-1/2″ (62x42 cm).
Large pen drawing on zinc.
5 artist reserved proofs.
50 signed and numbered proofs.
Zinc polished out.

85. LARGE PROFILE

April 2nd, 1947.
Format 24″x17″ (61x43,5 cm).
Rubbed crayon, pen and wash-drawing
on lithographic paper transferred to stone.
5 artist reserved proofs.
50 signed and numbered proofs.
Stone polished out.

86. STILL LIFE WITH STONEWARE POT

87. STILL LIFE WITH GLASS AND FLOWERS

86. STILL LIFE WITH STONEWARE POT

March 31st, 1947.
Format 23-3/4" x 17-1/4" (60 x 44 cm).
Worked lithographic paper, cut out and pasted
on to a lithographic crayon composition,
then transferred to stone.
Stamped in graded down black.
5 artist reserved proofs.
50 signed and numbered proofs.
Stone polished out.

87. STILL LIFE WITH GLASS AND FLOWERS

April 20th, 1947.
Format 21-1/4" x 15-1/4" (54 x 39 cm).
Wash drawing composition on zinc.
5 artist reserved proofs.
50 signed and numbered proofs.
Zinc polished out.

88. FIGURE

88. FIGURE

April 20th, 1947.
Format 29" x 22" (74 x 56 cm).
Ink and wash drawing composition on zinc.
5 artist reserved proofs.
Zinc preserved.

89. THE BLACK BULL

89. THE BLACK BULL

April 20th, 1947.
Format 23-1/4" x 15-3/4" (59 x 40 cm).
Wash drawing on zinc.
5 artist reserved proofs.
50 signed and numbered proofs.
Zinc polished out.

90. THE BLACK CUP

91. THE CUP AND THE APPLE

92. SMALL POT OF FLOWERS

90. THE BLACK CUP

April 21st, 1947.
Format 9-1/2"x6-1/4" (24x16 cm).
Small composition in scraped wash drawing
on lithographic paper transferred to stone.
Stone preserved.

91. THE CUP AND THE APPLE

April 21st, 1947.
Format 10"x6-1/4" (25x16 cm).
Still life in wash drawing on lithographic paper
transferred to stone.

92. SMALL POT OF FLOWERS

April 21st, 1947.
Format 9-1/2"x10-1/4" (24x26 cm).
Gouache worked wash drawing composition
on lithographic paper, transferred to stone.
4 trial proofs were made of these three lithographs.
Only Nos 91 and 92, of which 50 proofs,
pulled on Japan Hodomura paper,
were utilized in the set reserved
for the first 50 copies of the book
"Dans l'Atelier de Picasso" ("In Picasso's studio"),
Fernand Mourlot, publisher.

93. FLOWERS IN A GLASS No. 1

95. FLOWERS IN A GLASS No. 3

94. FLOWERS IN A GLASS No. 2

93. FLOWERS IN A GLASS No. 1

April 22nd, 1947. Format 9"x6" (23x15 cm).
Wash drawing with scrapings on
lithographic paper, transferred to stone.
4 trial proofs. Stone preserved.

94. FLOWERS IN A GLASS No. 2

April 22nd, 1947.
Format 9-1/2"x6-1/4" (24x16 cm).
Same process as for the preceding lithograph.
4 trial proofs. Stone preserved.

95. FLOWERS IN A GLASS No. 3

April 22nd, 1947.
Format 9-1/2"x6-1/4" (24x16 cm).
Gouache worked wash drawing on
lithographic paper transferred to stone.
4 trial proofs. Stone preserved.

96. FLOWERS IN A GLASS No. 4

98. FLOWERS IN A GLASS No. 6

97. FLOWERS IN A GLASS No. 5

96. FLOWERS IN A GLASS No. 4

April 22nd, 1947.
Format 9-1/2" x 6" (24 x 15 cm).
Same process as for the preceding lithograph.
4 trial proofs. Stone preserved.

97. FLOWERS IN A GLASS No. 5

April 22nd, 1947.
Format 9-1/2" x 6" (24 x 15 cm).
Gouache worked wash drawing on
lithographic paper, transferred to stone.
The wash drawing was executed
with an almost dry brush.   4 trial proofs.
50 proofs of this lithograph were made
on Japan Hodomura paper and were utilized in
the set reserved for the first fifty copies of the book
"Dans l'Atelier de Picasso", ("In Picasso's studio"),
Fernand Mourlot, publisher.

98. FLOWERS IN A GLASS No. 6

April 22nd, 1947. Format 9" x 6" (23 x 15 cm).
Gouache worked wash drawing
on lithographic paper transferred to stone.
This lithograph was utilized as a frontispiece
for Volume II of the four volume edition of the book
"Picasso lithographe" ("Picasso lithographs"),
André Sauret, publisher.
Format 9-1/2" x 12-1/2" (24,5 x 32 cm).
Run of 2,500 proofs. 10 artist reserved proofs.
Stone polished out.

99. FLOWERS IN A GLASS No. 7

100. SMALL NUDE FIGURE
SEATED AT THE MIRROR

99. FLOWERS IN A GLASS No. 7

April 22nd, 1947. Format 10″x6-1/4″ (25x16)
Wash drawing on lithographic paper.
4 trial proofs. Stone preserved.

100. SMALL NUDE FIGURE SEATED AT THE MIRROR

May 11th, 1947. Format 19″x12-1/4″ (48,5x31 cm).
Pen and brush drawing on lithographic paper,
transferred to stone. 5 artist reserved proofs.
50 signed and numbered proofs.
Stone polished out.

101. WOMEN ON THE BEACH

102. YOUNG NUDE WOMEN RESTING

101. WOMEN ON THE BEACH

May 11th, 1947.
Format 23-1/4" x 19-1/4" (59 x 49 cm).
Pen and brush composition on lithographic paper,
transferred to stone.
5 artist reserved proofs.
50 signed and numbered proofs.
Stone polished out.

102. YOUNG NUDE WOMEN RESTING

May 11th, 1947.
Format 24-1/2" x 19" (62 x 48 cm).
Pen drawing on lithographic paper,
transferred to stone.
5 artist reserved proofs.
50 signed and numbered proofs.
Stone polished out.

103. SEATED NUDE IN PROFILE

104. SEATED WOMAN
AND SLEEPING WOMAN

76

103. SEATED NUDE IN PROFILE

May 11th, 1947.
Format 23-3/4"x19" (60x48 cm).
Pen drawing on lithographic paper,
transferred to stone.
5 artist reserved proofs.
50 signed and numbered proofs.
Stone polished out.

104. SEATED WOMAN AND SLEEPING WOMAN

May 11th, 1947.
Format 19-1/4"x23-1/2" (49x60 cm).
2 colour composition in grey and black.
Wash drawing and crayon on zincs.
5 artist reserved proofs.
50 signed and numbered proofs.
Zincs polished out.

105. YOUNG WOMAN WITH TRIANGLE BODICE

106. HEAD OF YOUNG WOMAN

**105. YOUNG WOMAN WITH
TRIANGLE BODICE**

May 18th, 1947.
Format 21-1/4" x 17" (54 x 43 cm).
Crayon and gouache worked wash drawing
composition on lithographic paper
transferred to stone.
5 artist reserved proofs.
50 signed and numbered proofs.
Stone polished out.

106. HEAD OF YOUNG WOMAN

June 24th, 1947.
Format 23-1/2" x 17-3/4" (60 x 45 cm).
Wash drawing on zinc.
5 artist reserved proofs.
50 signed and numbered proofs.
Zinc polished out.

107. VASE OF FLOWERS WITH FLORAL
DESIGN CARPET

108. AUGUST 8th 1947 COMPOSITION

**107. VASE OF FLOWERS WITH FLORAL
DESIGN CARPET**

June 24th, 1947.
Format 24-1/2″x18″ (62x46 cm).
Rubbed crayon an a brush composition on zinc.
5 artist reserved proofs.
This plate could not be stamped, the zinc
having become oxidized before the stamping.

108. AUGUST 8th 1947 COMPOSITION

August 8th, 1947.
Format 19-3/4″x12-3/4″ (50x32,5 cm).
2 colour composition in black and ochre.
Wash drawing and paper cut out and pasted
on lithographic paper transferred to stone.
5 artist reserved proofs.
50 signed and numbered proofs.
Stones polished out.

1st state

109. DAVID AND BATHSHEBA

2nd state

109. DAVID AND BATHSHEBA
From the Lucas Cranach picture
(Berlin, Kaiser Friedrich Museum).

1st state. March 30th, 1947
Format of the composition
25-1/4" x 19-1/4" (64 x 49 cm).
Pen and wash drawing on zinc.
2nd state. Re-worked with pen
(many details added) and wash drawing; scrapings.

3rd state

109. DAVID AND BATHSHEBA

4th state

80

3rd state. The zinc is liberally spread with ink;
changes of details, scrapings.
4th state. The composition is completely re-inked
and re-drawn with a scraper.
5th state. A few faces cleared with scraper.

5th state

109. DAVID AND BATHSHEBA

6th state

6th state. March 30th, 1948.
After lying in a corner of the studio for almost one year the zinc
is re-worked by Picasso. Fine work with scraper.
Once again the plate is abandoned.
The zinc is extremely hard and has to be
deeply scraped so that the printer can ink
the plate without obliterating the fine lines.
The zinc has suffered serious damage
(Picasso's right hand has also suffered somewhat).
A transfer to stone is made from this last state without
polishing out the zinc, that old work companion.
There are therefore in the artist's studio, the zinc and the stone,
both well known to visitors, but for 6 months neither of them was touched.

7th state

109. DAVID AND BATHSHEBA

8th state

82

7th state. March 6th, 1949. The zinc is re-worked.
Few changes; scrapings in the faces
and in the upper part of the composition.
8th state. April 10th, 1949.
Some scrapings in the dress on the left,
the figures are re-drawn with ink.

9th state

109. DAVID AND BATHSHEBA

10th state

9th state. April 12th, 1949.
Complete change.
Picasso makes the plate as shiny as a mirror;
he must be fed up with scraping it.
He has removed everything from it
(probably with petrol),
but the engraving has left
the drawing visible, in grooves,
and he has re-drawn with pen on the zinc.
All the work has been successful.

10th state. April 17th, 1949.
Format 27-1/2" x 19-3/4" (70 x 50 cm).
Re-worked with wash drawing and scraper.
The composition is enlarged to the edges of the zinc.

5 artist reserved proofs of the 10 states
of this zinc were made.
Only the 1st, 2nd and 4th states were pulled
in 50 signed and numbered proofs.

At Picasso's request a transfer to stone
was made of the 6th state of the zinc.
Lithographic stone is much more
pleasant to work and especially
to scrape than zinc.
Taken to the artist's studio
in the Rue des Grands Augustins,
in November 1948, it was placed
on a large cast-iron cooking pot,
but Picasso seldom went near it.
"It frightens me, I dare not touch it",
he told me when I inquired about it.
However, the stone was attacked
once more, worked on and scraped;
one day some re-touching with a pen,
the next day a long session of scraping,
then a re-working of the blacks, etc.
Picasso would no doubt still be working
on it if, having to leave for the South
of France at the beginning of June 1949,
he had not asked that the stone be
removed and a proof pulled.
At present the stone is at the printing
works. I should be most surprised if
it did not go back to the artist's again
before being finally polished out.

84

109 (a). DAVID AND BATHSHEBA

109 (a). DAVID AND BATHSHEBA

Transfer to stone of the composition on zinc
of March 30th, 1948: 6th state.
1st state. May 9th, 1949.
Pen drawing, numerous scrapings.
On April 7th, 1949, the date engraved on the
bottom left of the composition, no proof was pulled.
5 trial proofs on paper 22" x 30" (56 x 76 cm)
reserved for the artist. Stone preserved.

Picasso left Paris for Golfe-Juan in Autumn 1947. While there he went every afternoon to the Ramié pottery works at Vallauris (a few kilometres from Golfe-Juan) where he worked without a break until evening.
But the publisher Tériade insisted that "The Song of the Dead" begun in 1945 but abandoned since then should be finished.
The zincs were despatched but the proofs of the wash drawings did not satisfy the artist and the zincs were polished out.
In March 1948 I took him some new zincs and, between two days at the pottery works, Picasso finished the book.
But there were 7 zincs too many and there was still some lithographic ink left; in the same day the 7 following compositions were made "The big owl" and the six Fauns, remarkable as compositions as well as lithographs.

110. THE BIG OWL

110. THE BIG OWL

Vallauris, March 10th, 1948.
Format 27" x 21" (68 x 53 cm).
Wash drawing on zinc, scraper.
5 artist reserved proofs.
50 signed and numbered proofs.
Zinc polished out.

111. PAN

112. SMILING FAUN

111. PAN

Vallauris, March 10th, 1948.
Format 25-1/2"x20" (65x51 cm).
Wash drawing on zinc.
5 artist reserved proofs.
50 signed and numbered proofs.
Zinc polished out.

112. SMILING FAUN

Vallauris, March 10th, 1948.
Format 26"x21" (66x53 cm).
Wash drawing on zinc.
5 artist reserved proofs.
50 signed and numbered proofs.
Zinc polished out.

114. MUSICIAN FAUN No. 3

113. FAUN WITH BRANCHES

113. FAUN WITH BRANCHES

Vallauris, March 10th, 1948.
Format 26" x 20-3/4" (66 x 52,5 cm).
Wash drawing on zinc.
5 artist reserved proofs.
50 signed and numbered proofs.
Zinc polished out.

114. MUSICIAN FAUN No. 3

Vallauris, March 10th, 1948.
Format 25-1/4" x 21" (64 x 53 cm).
Wash drawing on zinc.
5 artist reserved proofs.
50 signed and numbered proofs.
Zinc polished out.

116. MUSICIAN FAUN No. 5

115. MUSICIAN FAUN No. 4

115. MUSICIAN FAUN No. 4

Vallauris, March 10th, 1948.
Format 25-3/4" x 20-1/2" (65 x 52 cm).
Wash drawing on zinc.
5 artist reserved proofs.
50 signed and numbered proofs.
Zinc polished out.

116. MUSICIAN FAUN No. 5

Vallauris, March 10th, 1948.
Format 27" x 19-3/4" (69 x 50 cm).
Wash drawing on zinc.
5 artist reserved proofs.
50 signed and numbered proofs.
Zinc polished out.

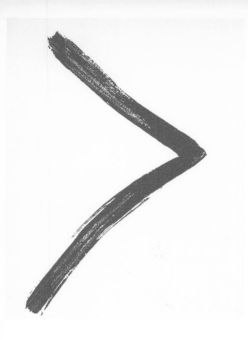

117. THE SONG OF THE DEAD

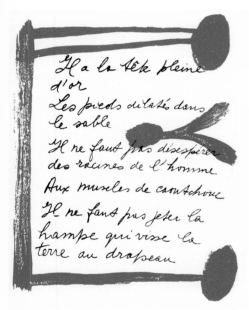

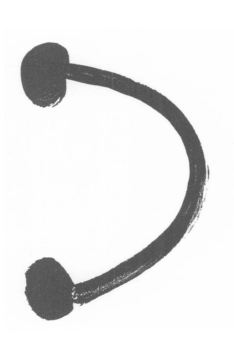

117. THE SONG OF THE DEAD

Poems by Pierre Reverdy, Tériade, publisher.
Format of book 16-1/2"x12-3/4" (42 x 32 cm).
250 proofs on Arches wove paper and
20 proofs not for sale. Reverdy's text
was reproduced by line plate manuscript size
and printed in letterpress by Draeger Frères.
Text illustrated with 125 Picasso lithographs:
2 for the cover and 123 for the poems.
Picasso began working in November 1945;
wash drawings printed in red, black
and red lithographs, wash drawings on paper.

All the trial illustrations, (reproduced under Nos.13,
14 and 15) were polished out immediately,
with the exception of one, No. 13.
The first arabesques were executed on stone
in January and February, 1946. In 1947,
Picasso made some new plates, on zinc,
at his own studio. Then, he finished the work
in the course of the winter 1947-48 on zincs
sent to him at Vallauris where he was working
on his pieces of pottery. But the inking
of the wash drawings produced
what we call a "toad skin" owing to oxidization
of the zinc and Picasso rejected

these compositions. The artist finished
his illustrations at Vallauris in March 1948.
All the zincs and all the stones have been
polished out. The composition on page 24
of the book had been transferred to stone before
the zinc was polished out and was utilized
by the Galerie Carré as a poster for the exhibition
of the book. December 1948.

118. FIRST VALLAURIS POSTER

Picasso had to make a lithograph
for utilization as poster for the
"Vallauris, Pieces of Pottery, Flowers, Perfumes"
Exhibition (24th-29th of August, 1948)
the 1,000 proofs of which were
to be offered to the Vallauris town. Finally, after
having produced three models (Nos. 118, 119, 120),
Picasso decided to print 300 copies of each of them.

118 (a)

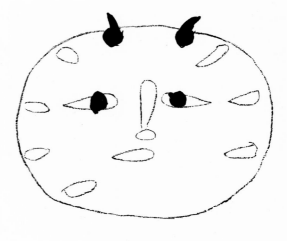

118 (b)

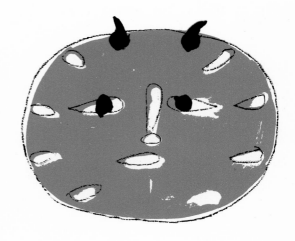

118. FIRST VALLAURIS POSTER

June 5th, 1948. Format of poster 15-3/4" x 23-3/4" (40 x 60 cm).
2 colour composition in wash drawing and crayon
on lithographic paper transferred to stone.
300 posters on Crèvecœur du Marais wove paper.

118 (a) Black line print of the first poster.
25 proofs on Arches paper 19-3/4" x 25-1/2" (50 x 65 cm)
signed and numbered.
118 (b) 2 colour composition.
25 proofs on Arches 19-3/4" x 25-1/2" (50 x 65 cm)
signed and numbered. Stones polished out.

119. SECOND VALLAURIS POSTER

119 (a)

119 (b)

119. SECOND VALLAURIS POSTER

June 5th, 1948. Format 15-3/4" x 23-1/2" (40 x 60 cm).
Scraped wash drawing, brush and rubbed crayon
on lithographic paper transferred to stone.
The paper was backed on a wood board
the asperities of which can be seen.
300 posters stamped on Crèvecœur wove paper.

119 (a). Black line print of the second poster.
25 proofs on Arches paper, 19-3/4" x 25-1/2" (50 x 65 cm),
signed and numbered. Stone polished out.
119 (b). 2 colour composition.
25 proofs on Arches paper, 19-3/4" x 25-1/2" (50 x 65 cm),
signed and numbered.

120. THIRD VALLAURIS POSTER

120 (a)

120 (b)

120. THIRD VALLAURIS POSTER

June 5th, 1948. Format 15-3/4" x 23-1/2" (40 x 60 cm).
Same process as for No. 119.
300 posters stamped on Crèvecœur wove paper.
Stone polished out.

120 (a). Black line print of the third poster.
25 proofs on Arches wove paper, 19-3/4" x 25-1/2" (50 x 65 cm),
signed and numbered.
120 (b). Composition in 2 colours.
25 proofs on Arches wove paper, 19-3/4" x 25-1/2" (50 x 65 cm),
signed and numbered.

*On his return to Paris Picasso plunged into work.
During his 8 month stay in Paris he did little
painting, but he made numerous compositions
on lithographic paper and on zinc.
Every day around 12 o' clock new plates had
to be collected, proofs from the previous
evening had to be brought and zincs prepared
for further alterations. "I am sorry to give you
this trouble. I would willingly work at your place,
but this would mean I should waste time..."
and Picasso continued working on his
lithographs without respite and with no regard
at all for the traditional rules. From time to time
he would visit his friends at Rue de Chabrol
and thank Raymond Tutin, the pressman who
worked for him and who often cursed his
lithographic oddities.*

121. CENTAUR DANCING, BLACK BACKGROUND

94

121. CENTAUR DANCING, BLACK BACKGROUND

October, 1948. Format 19-3/4" x 25-1/2" (50 x 65 cm).
Wash drawing and scrapings
on lithographic paper transferred to stone.
5 artist reserved proofs.
50 signed and numbered proofs.
Stone polished out.

122. HEAD OF WOMAN

123. BULL'S HEAD, turned to the left

124. BULL'S HEAD, turned to right

122. HEAD OF WOMAN

November 10th, 1948.
Format 17-1/4" x 24-1/2" (44 x 62 cm).
Large wash drawing on zinc.
5 artist reserved proofs. Zinc preserved.
No further proofs were pulled as the zinc was damaged.

123. BULL'S HEAD, turned to the left

Nov. 1948. Format 19-3/4" x 25-1/2" (50 x 65 cm).
Wash drawing and crayon on zinc.
5 artist reserved proofs.
50 signed and numbered proofs. Zinc polished out.

124. BULL'S HEAD, turned to right

Nov. 1948. Format 19-3/4" x 25-1/2" (50 x 65 cm).
Ink and crayon composition on lithographic paper,
transferred to stone. 5 artist reserved proofs.
50 signed and numbered proofs. Stone polished out.

125. THE STUDIO

126. BLACK FIGURE

96

125. THE STUDIO

November 10th, 1948.
Format 19" x 24" (48 x 61 cm).
Crayon, pen and wash drawing composition on zinc
showing a corner of the studio
in the Rue des Grands Augustins.
5 artist reserved proofs.
50 signed and numbered proofs.
Zinc polished out.

126. BLACK FIGURE

November 20th, 1948.
Format 19-3/4" x 25-1/2" (50 x 65 cm).
Flat black on zinc cleared with glass paper and
scraper, the lower part of the bodice, the neck
and the ear were preserved
and worked on with crayon.
5 artist reserved proofs.
50 signed and numbered proofs.
Zinc polished out.

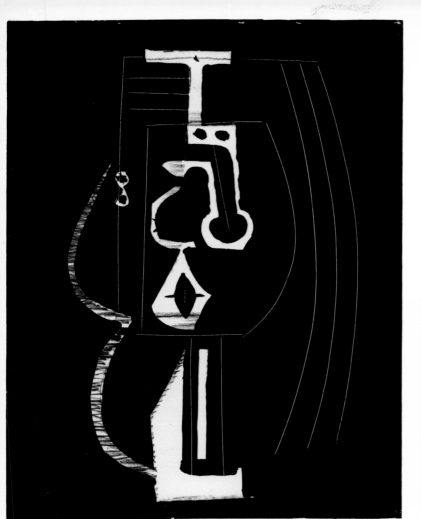

127. COMPOSITION

128. FIGURE

127. COMPOSITION

November 21st, 1948.
Format 19-3/4″ x 25-1/4″ (50 x 64 cm).
Crayon, flat tint ink and scraper composition on zinc
5 artist reserved proofs.
50 signed and numbered proofs.
Zinc polished out.

128. FIGURE

November 21st, 1948.
Format 19-3/4″ x 25-1/2″ (50 x 65 cm).
Crayon and rubbings, ink and scrapings,
composition on zinc.
5 artist reserved proofs.
50 signed and numbered proofs.
Zinc polished out.

129. FIGURE

130. FIGURE

98

129. FIGURE

November 21st, 1948.
Format 18-1/2" x 24-1/2" (47 x 62 cm).
Flat ink and rubbed crayon on zinc.
5 artist reserved proofs.
50 signed and numbered proofs.
Zinc polished out.

130. FIGURE

November 21st, 1948.
Format 19-3/4" x 25-1/2" (50 x 65 cm).
Flat ink, scrapings and rubbed crayon on zinc.
5 artist reserved proofs.
50 signed and numbered proofs.
Zinc polished out.

1st state

131. STYLIZED FIGURE

2nd state

131. STYLIZED FIGURE

1st state. November 21st, 1948.
Format 19-3/4" x 25-1/2" (50 x 65 cm).
Flat ink, crayon and scraper on zinc.
2nd state. December 13th, 1948.
Work with added crayon, numerous white lines
with scraper, the figure, right hand part,
is transformed, benzin removed, and re-drawn.

131. STYLIZED FIGURE

3rd state

100

6.12.48.

132. PROFILES STUDY

131. STYLIZED FIGURE

3rd state. December 21st, 1948.
New transformation, principally executed
by background removal.
5 artist reserved proofs of these three states
were pulled. 1 proof of the second and third states
was pulled on Annam mulberry paper
(Mûrier d'Annam).
50 numbered and signed proofs of the third state.
Zinc polished out.

132. PROFILES STUDY

December 8th, 1948.
Format 21-1/4" x 38-3/4" (54 x 73 cm).
Series of pen and brush drawings,
crayon rubbings to try a paper sized according to
the artist's guiding rules; transfer to zinc.
Zinc polished out.

103

One proof of each of these colours
having been pulled separately,
we have been able to reconstitute the lithograph
such as it should have been pulled
in large dimensions with the exact tints required.
Here is this hitherto "unknown" lithograph.

133 (a). THE ARMCHAIR WOMAN

2nd state

104

133 (a). THE ARMCHAIR WOMAN

2nd state. Each zinc has been re-worked:
crayon, ink, scrapings. New proofing with colours.
The result is not yet satisfactory.
The plates are again put into condition
for new corrections, but each colour will be
transformed in a black plate
and the 5 new compositions will be the object
of more or less developed studies.
Each day or each night the zincs will be scraped,
polished out, re-drawn, as we shall see
in the following plates.

1st state

134. ARMCHAIR WOMAN No. 1 (from the red)

2nd state

134. ARMCHAIR WOMAN No. 1 (from the red)

1st state. December 10th, 1948.
On the plate of the red second state, ink flats added,
brush, crayon, scrapings.
2nd state. December 13th, 1948.
Scrapings with glass paper and needle, crayon, ink.
The following states will be worked on
in the same way.

3rd state

134. ARMCHAIR WOMAN No. 1 (from the red)

4th state

3rd state. December 15th, 1948.
4th state. December 17th, 1948.
5th state. December 20th, 1948.
A transfer of this state on another zinc is made
and a reproduction proof on a new plate,
but Picasso still retouches
the original zinc in a 6th state.
Zinc preserved.
6th state. December 23rd, 1948.
The features are purified; cleaning of the background
The plate is abandoned after this state.

5th state

134. ARMCHAIR WOMAN No. 1 (from the red)

6th state

1st state

134. ARMCHAIR WOMAN No. 1 (from the red)

2nd state of transfer

1st state. From the December 20th transfer.
December 23rd, 1948.
Changes and details added with pen.
After the proofs of this state,
Picasso has transformed
the composition in a plate with colours.
The face is filled up with ink and the plate will
serve as grey tint.
2nd state of transfer. January 13th, 1949.
The grey having been done away with,
the zinc is re-worked, face drawn with pen.

3rd state of transfer

134. ARMCHAIR WOMAN No. 1 (from the red)

Final state

3rd state of transfer. January 16th, 1949.
Not much change; the zinc is put aside.
Zinc preserved.

Final state.
On the reproduction proof of December 20th
and in view of the plate with colours,
Picasso completes in a masterly manner
the composition of December 30th.
The superimposition of the 2 colours, page 110,
does not entirely satisfy him and the black only
will be pulled.
5 proofs of each of all these states are pulled;
50 numbered and signed proofs of the final state
are pulled. Zinc polished out. .

134. ARMCHAIR WOMAN No. 1

Superimposition of the two colours

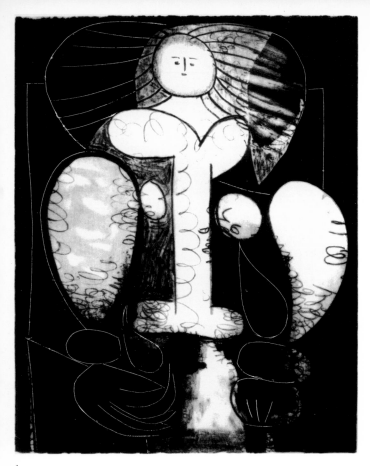

1st state

2nd state

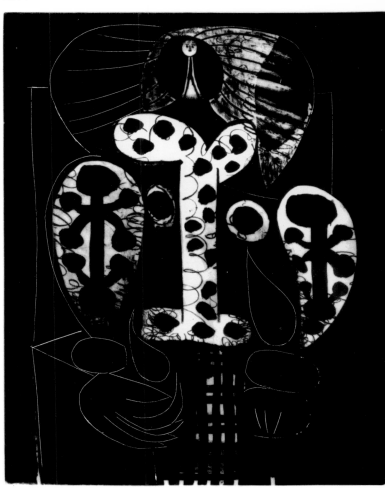

135. ARMCHAIR WOMAN No. 2 (from the green)

1st state. December 10th, 1948. 5 proofs.
2nd state. April 5th, 1949. 5 proofs.

1st state

136. ARMCHAIR WOMAN No. 3 (from the yellow)

2nd state

136. ARMCHAIR WOMAN No. 3 (from the yellow)

1st state. December 10th, 1948. 5 proofs.
2nd state. April 5th 1949. 5 proofs.

112

1st state

137. ARMCHAIR WOMAN No. 4 (from the violet)

2nd state

137. ARMCHAIR WOMAN No. 4 (from the violet)

1st state. December 10th, 1948.
2nd state. December 16th, 1948.

3rd state

137. ARMCHAIR WOMAN No. 4 (from the violet)

4th state

3rd state. December 22nd, 1948.
A transfer of this state has been effected.
4th state. December 26th, 1948.
5th state. January 3rd 1949.
Rubbing of the whites with glass paper,
the features are purified,
the black flats lined with ink.
The plate is abandoned.

5th state

137. ARMCHAIR WOMAN No. 4 (from the violet)

1st state of transfer

115

1st state of transfer. December 28th, 1948.
From the transfer of December 22nd, erasures;
new personage drawing.

137. ARMCHAIR WOMAN No. 4

(from the violet)

2nd state of transfer : January 2nd, 1949.
New transformation, then the zinc is left waiting.
5 artist reserved proofs have been pulled of each
of the 7 states of this composition.

1st state

138. ARMCHAIR WOMAN (from the black)

2nd state

138. ARMCHAIR WOMAN (from the black)

1st state. Served as black for the plate
with colours 1st state (No. 133).
2nd state. Served as black for the plate
with colours 2nd state (No. 133 (a)).

3rd state

138. ARMCHAIR WOMAN (from the black)

4th state

3rd state. November 23rd, 1948.
4th state. December 4th, 1948.
5th state. December 11th, 1948.
6th state. December 17th, 1948
After this state the plate is abandoned.
From the 3rd state to the 6th state,
5 artist reserved proofs
of each state have been made;
the 2 first states were utilized for pulling proofs
only with the colour plates.

6th state

5th state

1st state

2nd state

120

139. THE TABLE WITH FISH

Picasso wants a change of subject;
he abandons one after the other the different states
of the "Armchair woman"
and produces two large still-life
compositions with fish.
1st state. December 17th 1948.
Format 27-1/2" x 21-1/2" (70 x 54,5 cm).
Large composition executed in
wash drawing on zinc.

2nd state. December 21st, 1948.
Wash drawing and crayon added;
a third fish appears, and a sea-urchin
is transformed into a drinking-glass.

3rd state

139. THE TABLE WITH FISH

4th state

3rd state. December 26th, 1948.
Scrapings with glass paper, brush and pen added.
4th state. December 30th, 1948.
Erasures and scrapings with glass paper,
the zinc rubbed parts are shining and the plate,
before being prepared for inking,
looks like bright silver.

5th state

139. THE TABLE WITH FISH

140. TABLE WITH FISH, BLACK BACKGROUND

122

139. THE TABLE WITH FISH

5th state, January 7th, 1949.
Details with pen and brush
and then the plate is abandoned.
5 artist reserved proofs of each of these states.
Zinc preserved.

140. TABLE WITH FISH, BLACK BACKGROUND

1st state. December 17th, 1948.
Format 27-1/2" x 21-1/2" (70 x 54,5 cm).
Wash drawing on zinc.
2nd state. December 21st, 1948.
The wash drawing is everywhere reinforced and,
after this state, the proof of which does not please
him much, Picasso abandons this composition.
5 proofs of each of these 2 states.

141. THE DOVE

2nd state

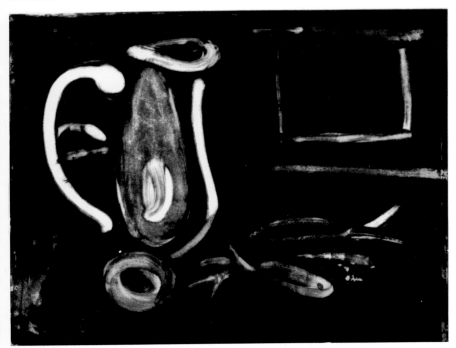

123

141. THE DOVE

January 9th, 1949.
Format 27-1/2" x 21-1/2" (70 x 54,5 cm). Wash drawing on zinc.
This composition is one of the most beautiful lithos ever produced;
the mellowness obtained in the plumage,
of which our reproduction evokes only a faint idea,
is absolutely remarkable. This plate (with Nos. 142, 143 and 144)
gets the maximum of what can be obtained with litho ink utilized in
wash drawing. 5 artist reserved proofs. 50 numbered and signed proofs.
Zinc polished out. Thousands of copies of this dove were used
as an illustration of the Peace Congress Poster (April 1949).

142. LOBSTERS AND FISH

124

142. LOBSTERS AND FISH

January 7th, 1949.
Format 29-1/2" x 41-1/2" (75 x 105 cm).
Wash drawing on zinc.
Remarkable composition both for
the quality of its wash drawings and for its dimensions.
5 artist reserved proofs.
Run of 50 numbered and signed proofs.
Zinc polished out.

143. THE LOBSTER

144. THE TOAD

126

143. THE LOBSTER

January 9th, 1949.
Format 27-1/2" x 21-1/2" (70 x 54,5 cm).
Wash drawing on zinc.
5 artist reserved proofs.
50 numbered and signed proofs.
Zinc polished out.

144. THE TOAD

January 13th, 1949.
Format 19-1/2" x 25-1/4" (49,5 x 64 cm).
Wash drawing on zinc.
5 artist reserved proofs.
50 numbered and signed proofs.
Zinc polished out.

1st state

145. HEAD OF YOUNG GIRL

127

145. HEAD OF YOUNG GIRL

1st state. January 11th, 1949.
Format 19-1/2" x 25-1/4" (49,5 x 64 cm).
The last wash drawings becoming too facile
and with a too certain result;
Picasso tries another technique.
The obtained half tones show off a fine mellowness.
2nd state. January 14th, 1949.
Re-working with crayon and wash drawing.

3rd state

145. HEAD OF YOUNG GIRL

4th state

128

145. HEAD OF YOUNG GIRL

3rd state. March 9th, 1949.
Scrapings with glass-paper.
4th state. March 16th, 1949.
Erasures with glass paper, crayon and brush added.
5 artist reserved proofs of each of these 4 states.
Zinc preserved.

146. STILL-LIFE WITH VASE OF FLOWERS

1st state

2nd state

146. STILL-LIFE WITH VASE OF FLOWERS

1st state. January 13th, 1949.
Format 19-1/2″×12-1/2″ (49,5×64 cm).
Picasso takes up the technique already tried out
for the preceding number. The result is interesting
for the quality of the background.
2nd state. January 16th, 1949.
All the values are reinforced. But Picasso,
who practically does not stop working, produces
too much for a single pressman, however the best ;
it is necessary to call for a second printer, less skilful,
who deteriorates the plate. 5 proofs of these two states.

148. YOUNG WOMAN

147. HEAD OF YOUNG GIRL

1st state   *2nd state*

149. HEAD OF A YOUNG GIRL

147. HEAD OF YOUNG GIRL

January 16th, 1949.
Format 15-1/2" x 11-3/4" (39,5 x 30 cm).
Search for a new technique on zinc.
5 trial proofs.   Zinc preserved.

148. YOUNG WOMAN

January 16th, 1949.
Format 15-1/2" x 11-3/4" (39,5 x 30 cm).
New wash drawing trials on zinc, pen.
5 trial proofs. Zinc preserved.

149. HEAD OF A YOUNG GIRL

1st state. February 13th, 1949.
Format 14-1/2" x 11-3/4" (36,5 x 30 cm).
Wash drawing on zinc. 5 trial proofs.
2nd state. February 17th, 1949.
5 trial proofs.
Run of 50 numbered and signed proofs.
Zinc polished out.

150. THE YOUNG ARTIST

1st state   *2nd state*

151. PORTRAIT OF YOUNG GIRL   152. SECOND PORTRAIT OF YOUNG GIRL

150. THE YOUNG ARTIST

1st state. February 17th, 1949.
Format 15-1/2" x 11-3/4" (39,5 x 30 cm).
Composition with pen and wash drawing.
5 trial proofs.
2nd state. April 14th, 1949.
Numerous details added with pen. 5 trial proofs.
Run of 50 numbered and signed proofs.
Zinc polished out.

151. PORTRAIT OF YOUNG GIRL

February 16th, 1949.
Format 15-1/2" x 11-3/4" (39,5 x 30 cm).
Wash drawing and pen on zinc.
5 trial proofs. Zinc preserved.

152. SECOND PORTRAIT OF YOUNG GIRL

February 16th, 1949.
Format 15-1/2" x 11-3/4" (39,5 x 30 cm).
Replica of the preceding number, same process.
5 trial proofs. Zinc preserved.

153. YOUNG WOMAN

132

153. YOUNG WOMAN

February 17th, 1949.
Format 15-1/2" x 11-3/4" (39,5 x 30 cm).
Wash drawing on zinc. 5 trial proofs.
Run of 100 proofs on Arches wove paper
for the Centenary Album
of the Mourlot Printing Works, 1952.
In the composition, lower right part,
the artist has written on a red printed zinc:
"Pour le Centenaire de Mourlot-Picasso"
("For the Centenary of Mourlot-Picasso").

154. THE ARMCHAIR WOMAN (variante)

Composition obtained by the pulling of the second
state of transfer No. 137, within which was reserved
the space for the No. 153 litho, pulled in second.
Picasso is much interested in this trial, requested
by him, and at this time, inspired by this idea,
he does two paintings on canvas. 5 proofs.

155. HEAD OF YOUNG GIRL

156. THE ARTIST AND THE CHILD

155. HEAD OF YOUNG GIRL

February 17th, 1949.
Format 15-1/2" x 12" (39,5 x 30 cm).
Wash drawing on zinc.
5 trial proofs. Zinc preserved.

156. THE ARTIST AND THE CHILD

February 20th, 1949.
Format 25" x 18-1/2" (63 x 47 cm).
Composition with pen on zinc.
5 artist reserved proofs. Zinc preserved.

1st state

157. YOUNG GIRL WITH STRIPED BODICE

2nd state

134

157. YOUNG GIRL WITH STRIPED BODICE

1st state. February 26th, 1949.
Format 25" x 18-3/4" (63 x 48 cm).
Composition with crayon,
wash drawing and pen on zinc.
2nd state. March 4th, 1949. Scrapings, ink added.
5 proofs of each state. Zinc preserved.

1st state

158. BUST OF YOUNG WOMAN

2nd state

158. BUST OF YOUNG WOMAN

1st state. February 26th, 1949.
Format 24-1/2" x 18-3/4" (62 x 48 cm).
Wash drawing, crayon and brush on zinc.
2nd state. March 4th, 1949.
The upper part of the head of hair is cleared.
5 proofs of each state. Zinc preserved.

159. COVER PROJECT

160. COVER MOURLOT I

159. COVER PROJECT

March 6th, 1949.
Format 27-1/2"x21" (70x53,5 cm).
Composition on zinc executed
as a cover for the 1st tome of the four volume
edition of the book "Picasso lithographs".
Picasso amused himself drawing in the margins.
5 artist reserved proofs. Zinc preserved.

160. COVER MOURLOT I

March 5th, 1949.
Format 19-3/4"x12-1/2" (50x32 cm).
Composition with wash drawing on zinc,
litho crayon drawing, scrapings with glass paper.
Served as a cover for the 1st tome of the book
"Picasso lithographs" four volume edition,
format 9-3/4"x12-1/2" (24,5x32 cm).
Run of 2,500 copies. André Sauret, Publisher.
5 artist reserved proofs. Zinc polished out.

161. WHITE BUST ON BLACK

161. WHITE BUST ON BLACK

March 4th, 1949.
Format 23-1/4"x17-1/4" (59x44 cm).
Drawing with white gouache on ink coated
litho paper and transferred to stone.
5 trial proofs. 50 numbered and signed proofs.
Stone polished out.

162. FIGURE

March 4th, 1949.
Format 25-1/2"x19-3/4" (65x50 cm).
Wash drawing and crayon on litho paper
transferred to stone. 5 trial proofs.
Run of 50 numbered and signed proofs.
Stone polished out.

163. BUST WITH STAR SPANGLED BACKGROUND

164. MODERN STYLE BUST

138

163. BUST WITH STAR SPANGLED BACKGROUND

Dated April 7th, 1949 but in reality March 7th, 1949.
Format 19-3/4" x 25-1/2" (50 x 65 cm).
Worked with gouache wash drawing
transferred to stone.
7 artist reserved proofs, of which 2 blue ones.
50 numbered and signed proofs.
Stone polished out.

164. MODERN STYLE BUST

March 8th, 1949.
Format 19-3/4" x 25-1/2" (50 x 65 cm).
Wash drawing and gouache on litho paper
transferred to stone. These two lithos (163 and 164)
with wash drawing on paper are,
from the professional point of view,
a remarkable success.
5 artist reserved proofs.
50 numbered and signed proofs.
Stone polished out.

165. COMPOSED FIGURE I

166. COMPOSED FIGURE II

165. COMPOSED FIGURE I

March 8th, 1949.
Format 19-3/4" x 25-1/2" (50 x 65 cm).
Wash drawing and gouache on litho paper
transferred to stone.
5 artist reserved proofs.
50 numbered and signed proofs.
Stone polished out.

166. COMPOSED FIGURE II

March 8th, 1949.
Format 19-3/4" x 25-1/2" (50 x 65 cm).
Same process as for No. 165.
5 trial proofs. 50 numbered and signed proofs.

167. THE BULL'S RETURN

168. THE GREAT BULLFIGHT

167. THE BULL'S RETURN

December 1945.
Format 10-1/4″ x 6″ (26 x 15 cm).
Scraped litho ink flat, cut and pasted on a litho paper
and transferred to stone.
A single proof on ordinary paper.
Stone polished out.

168. THE GREAT BULLFIGHT

1st state. March 11th, 1949.
Format 21-1/2″ x 26-1/2″ (55 x 67 cm).
Composition on litho paper, crayon and
wash drawing transferred to stone.
5 artist reserved proofs.
Run of 50 numbered and signed proofs.
Stone polished out.

169. THE GREAT BULLFIGHT II

170. THE GREAT BULLFIGHT III

169. THE GREAT BULLFIGHT II

2nd state. March 21st, 1949.
Format 21-1/2″ x 27″ (55 x 69 cm).
The stone of No. 168 serves as grey background
and a new black on zinc is executed
and pulled in second.
5 trial proofs.

170. THE GREAT BULLFIGHT III

March 31st, 1949.
Format 21-1/2″ x 27″ (55 x 69 cm).
The black of No. 169 is re-worked
with pen and wash drawing;
the grey is suppressed.
5 trial proofs. Zinc preserved.

171. THE BANDERILLAS

172. BULLFIGHT . THE PICADOR

142

171. THE BANDERILLAS

April 25th, 1949.
Format 19" x 21-1/2" (48 x 55 cm).
Wash drawing worked with gouache on litho paper
transferred to stone.
5 trial proofs. Run of 50 numbered and signed proofs.
Stone polished out.

172. BULLFIGHT . THE PICADOR

March 11th, 1949.
Format 21-1/4" x 26" (54 x 66 cm).
Crayon, gouache and wash drawing on litho paper
transferred to stone.
The plate indicates : 11/3/49 - March 15th, 1949.
5 trial proofs. Run of 50 numbered
and signed proofs. Stone polished out.

173. SMALL PIGEON

174. THE SMALL DOVE

143

173. SMALL PIGEON

March 1949.
Format 7-3/4″ x 10″ (20 x 25 cm).
Wash drawing executed on newsprint paper
and transferred to stone. 5 trial proofs.
Stone preserved.

174. THE SMALL DOVE

March 1949. Format 8-1/4″ x 10-1/4″ (21 x 26 cm).
Wash drawing with litho ink
on newsprint paper transferred to stone.
15 artist reserved proofs.
This litho served as frontispiece to the 1st tome
of the four volume edition of "Picasso lithographs",
run executed on the transfer stone,
in format 9-3/4″ x 12-1/2″ (24,5 x 32 cm).
Run of 2,500 copies. André Sauret, Publisher.
Stone polished out.

175. THE CHECK CLOTH BODICE

175 (a). THE CHECK CLOTH BODICE

176. YOUNG GIRL INSPIRED BY CRANACH

144

175. THE CHECK CLOTH BODICE

March 26th, 1949.
Format 19-3/4" x 25-1/2" (50 x 65 cm).
Composition with wash drawing and ink on
litho paper already impressed with litho Nos. 163;
transfer to stone. Rose colour printing of No. 163
and superimposition of black.
5 trial proofs. 50 numbered and signed black prints.
Stone polished out.

175 (a). THE CHECK CLOTH BODICE

March 26th, 1949. Format 19-3/4" x 25-1/2" (50 x 65).
Printing of the black stone. 5 artist reserved proofs.
50 numbered and signed proofs.

176. YOUNG GIRL INSPIRED BY CRANACH

March 26th-27th, 1949.
Format 19-3/4" x 25-1/2" (50 x 65 cm).
Composition with litho ink and gouache on litho paper
transferred to stone. 5 artist reserved proofs.
25 numbered and signed proofs.

163 (a). ROSE COLOUR BACKGROUND

176 (a). YOUNG GIRL INSPIRED BY CRANACH

163 (a). ROSE COLOUR BACKGROUND

March 28th, 1949.
Format 19-3/4" x 25-1/2" (50 x 65 cm).
Litho No. 163 has been scraped according to
a tracing of No. 176 and will serve
as a second colour for the plate No. 176 (a).

176 (a). YOUNG GIRL INSPIRED BY CRANACH

March 26th-27th, 1949.
Format 19-3/4" x 25-1/2" (50 x 65 cm).
Plates Nos. 176 and 163 (a) are register
printed in rose colour and black.
5 artist reserved proofs.
25 numbered and signed proofs.
Stones polished out.

177. HYPETONGA ELEGY

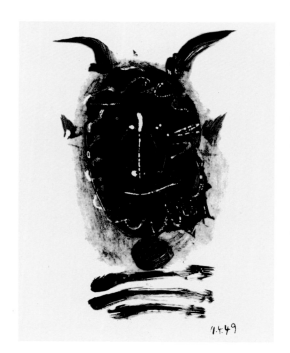

177. HYPETONGA ELEGY

Yvan Goll's Poems. Edition Hémisphères, Paris.
April 11th, 1949.
Format 12-3/4"x10" (32,2 x 25 cm).
4 lithographs. Wash drawing on litho paper
transferred to stones.
20 proofs printed with follow up on Japan paper,
180 proofs on Rives Paper,
plus 20 proofs not for sale. Stones polished out.

1er état   *1st state*

178. GREEN HAIRED WOMAN

1st state. March 28th, 1949.
Format 25-1/2" x 19-3/4" (65 x 50 cm).
4 colour lithograph; green, violet, bistre and black.
Wash drawing on litho paper transferred to zinc.
5 trial proofs.

178 (a). GREEN HAIRED WOMAN

2nd state. April 18th, 1949.
The 4 zincs have been retouched;
no change in the colour range.
5 trial proofs.

178 (b). GREEN HAIRED WOMAN

148

178 (b). GREEN HAIRED WOMAN

3rd state of black. May 30th, 1949.
The black plate only has been re-worked
and no colour proofs have been printed.
The 3 dates of the different states
can be clearly seen on the plate.
5 trial proofs. 50 numbered and signed proofs.
Zinc polished out.

178 (a). THE WOMAN WITH A HAIR NET

September 1956.
It appeared in the 2nd tome of the four volume edition
"Picasso lithographs", André Sauret, Publisher,
under the title "Green haired Woman" (No. 178 too)
Format 19-3/4" x 26" (50 x 66 cm).
4th state of the black.
Retouching on zinc of the green colour.
5 artist reserved proofs.
50 numbered and signed proofs.

179. FIGURE
WITH STRIPED BODICE

179. FIGURE WITH STRIPED BODICE

April 3rd, 1949. Format 25-1/2" x 19-3/4" (65 x 50 cm).
Litho in 6 colours: yellow, green, red, bistre, violet, black on stones.
Wash drawing on paper transferred to stone.
The artist has done this plate from one of his paintings
but he had no time to prepare a second state,
and this litho, like the preceding one, has been abandoned
on account of his departure for the south of France.
5 trial proofs. 50 numbered and signed proofs.
Stones polished out.

Look at these images: what variety, and what a diversity of techniques has been used. I have just spent a few days at Cannes and was received several times at the artist's studio; I was able to admire his recent works: paintings, ceramics, engravings, lithos, all of an exceptional quality. I saw a Picasso in "splendid form" younger and more cheerful than ever: he is working; therefore all is right for him.

180. POEMS AND LITHOGRAPHS
(Fragments of a Picasso text)

This set of 30 compositions and of 26 pages
of manuscript texts was completed by Picasso
between April 6th to May 29th, 1949.
The dates appear on most of the lithos,
but they do not follow the chronological order.
In fact, Picasso carried out his compositions
with litho ink, pen, wash drawing,
litho crayon and gouache on cut transfer papers
of the format 10" x 12-1/2" (25 x 32 cm).
He then assembled them in sets of 4,
not always following the chronological order.
Only litho III, "Two women",
of May 13th, 1949 is printed in the second state
of May 27th, 1949 (above page 15 of the book).
The plate of May 25th, 1949 near page 25
"Woman's head of hair"
has been retouched by the artist.
This album is composed of 14 plates
of format 19-3/4" x 25-1/2" (50 x 65 cm).
50 numbered copies were printed plus one for the artist
and one for the printer on Arches paper.
The Picasso copy comprises the proofs
on parchment and Japan paper.
This album is presented without title,
but with a colophon and with a cloth lined back board.
Galerie Louise Leiris, publisher, 1954.
The litho "Two nude women"
is printed in the second state (May 27th, 1949).
The "Back view of head of hair"
has been retouched by the artist.
All the other plates without correction.

180. POEMS AND LITHOGRAPHS

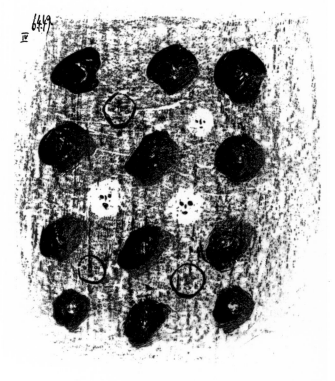

152

180. POEMS AND LITHOGRAPHS

180. POEMS AND LITHOGRAPHS

16.5.49. IV

16.5.49. III

LES SONS DES CLOCHETTES ATTACHÉES AUX
CERCLES ENCHANTÉS A MILLE LIEVES A LA RONDE ET SES
CRIS ENFERMÉS DANS L'ASSIETTE BOUILLANTE DE TOUT
SON BLEU AUX FEVILLES CHENVES DE SES BRAS SANGLE
VENTRE CREUX DE LA ROBE D'APPARAT ET DES BIJOUX
ETERMIES DANS L'ETANG D'OCRE PIÉTINÉ PAR LES
SABOTS DU JOVRINCLUS DANS L'ORDRE ET LES
MESVRES PRISES SUR LE FAIT A PRIORI REMPLI DE
PRÉCAVTIONS - FLVTES DE PAN ODORANTES
ET TOUTES CHAVDES PEIGNANT DU CARAMEL
DE SES CHEVEVX L'HEVRE QVI FOND GOUTTE A
GOUTTE SVR LES ÉPAVLES NUES DES LONGVES
TRESSES EMMÉLÉES REMPLISSANT LE VASE
PLEIN DE FLEVRS TAPANT DES POINGS SUR
LA PIERRE DU MIROIR LÉCHANT LE SANG FIGÉ
REFLÉTÉ EN SIGNES CONVENUS SUR L'ARDOISE
ACCAPARANT LA SCÈNE DE SES BAISERS 13.8.41
DE PEU A PROU LES GIRANDOLES ÉTONNÉES
DES ONGLES LIQVIDES DU SOIR QVI ÉCLATENT
AUX OREILLES AVEVGLES DES LEVRES ENTREOVVERTES
DES FENÊTRES PENDVES AUX LUMIÈRES RECOUVRENT
DE LEVRS LANGVES LES SOUPIRS ET LES PLUS MENVS
MAVVES DE L'ODEUR DE JASMINS CACHÉS AV FOND
DE LA MARE DE LAIT TIÈDE ET SVCRÉ ÉCLABOUSSANT
LE MANTEAV DE VELOVRS ACCROCHÉ'A LA
POINTE DE L'ÉPÉE AGITANT SES BRAS
DANS LA BLESSVRE OVVERTE DU MVR PEINT A LA
CHAVX

5.

ROBE MISE EN LAMBEAUX CHEVEUX
DÉFAITS TORDANT SA CHAIR JOUANT
AU JEU DE GRACE AVEC SES SEINS LES PLVS
ET LES RIDES DES VOILES - LA SALIVE DE SON
PARFVM LA COVRONNE DE CLOUS DE GIROFLE DU
CORSAGE MORDORÉ DE SES CILS LA LAINE NOIRE
DE SES MOVVEMENTS SON RIRE LE CHOC
MÉTALLIQVE DU COTON ET DU BEVRRE FRAIS
DE SES MAINS SES SAVTS DE CABRI ET LA
LONGVEVR DU TEMPS QVI SVINTE DU CIEL LES
CORDONS DE FAITS DE SON REGARD EMMÉLÉS
AVX FLEVRS DES MVRIERS ENTOURANT LE POIDS
CHAMP OVBLIÉ SUR LA COMMODE LE POIDS
DE LA POIX COLLÉE AUX AILES DU COEUR CLOVANT
SES DENTS DE TOUT LE PLOMB DE SON CORPS
DANS LE BOL DE TISANNE LES FLEVRS DU
BOUQUET MISES AUX FERS AU FOND DE LA
CALE DU MIROIR DE L'ARMOIRE A GLACE
LE MORCEAV DE PAAP DÉCHIRÉ PAR LE
SOLEIL QVI RENTRE A GROS BOUILLONS PAR
L'ÉGOUT DU BONHEVR CLAQUANT LE RIRE DE SES
COUPS DE FOUET SUR LE DOS NV
OU PLAFOND SES JEUX D'ADRESSE SES
MANIGANCES SES ALLURES DÉMESVRÉES
DE REINE SES PIEDS TOUCHANT A PEINE
L'EAV ET L'ORCHESTRE CELESTE PUANT
LES ROSES GRIMPANTES DE SES AIRS
AVX ANGLES DE L'ALCOVE VERS LVISANTS

6.

154

180. POEMS AND LITHOGRAPHS

DES LAMPES DE POUSSIERE FUYANT LA CATASTROPHE
LA MANIERE DE S'EN SERVIR RESTANT CACHÉE DERRIERE
LA TOILE - LA PORTE QUI S'OUVRE ACCOURT A L'APPEL
ET SE JETTE HALLETANTE DANS LES BRAS ÉTENDUS
QUI L'ATTENDENT. LA FACE PLEINE DE LARMES GRIMACE
LE BONHEUR LES MAINS SECOUENT LE SANG DU VOYAGE
COLLÉ AUX SANDALES LES GENOUX EN MONTANT GRIFFENT
A CHAQUE MARCHE LA PIERRE LE DIAMANT EFFRITE
SES DENTS SUR LE MIEL DE LA SOIE TENDUE LE MATIN
A NEUF HEURES SUR L'AUBE TOUTE NUE FRISSONNANTE
LE LIT OUVRE SES FEUILLES FUIS L'AVENIR LES LONGUES
ET COMPLIQUÉES ARABESQUES COLLÉES AUX SILENCES RETENUS
PAR LES PANS DE LEURS ROBES AUX ÉPINES DES RIDEAUX
BRÛLENT L'ENCENS LA MYRRHE ET LE BENJOIN AUX
PORTES FERMÉES LUISANTES DE VITRES - UN CHEVAL
BLANC VA DE FENETRE EN FENÊTRE 21.3.41. RIDEAUX DE
TULLE DÉCHIRANT LE CŒUR SUR LA SOIE BLEUE
DES BERGERES EN ÉTOUFFANT LES CRIS DE LARMES
AU FOND DES GORGES REBONDIES 30.4.41. LA CASSEROLE
PLEINE DE FIGUES DÉBORDANTE D'ESCARGOTS ET DES
FEUX D'ARTIFICE CRACHÉS A PLEINES MAINS ÉCLABOU-
SSANT DE TOUS SES JETS LES PIERRES ARRONDIES
TAPPANT À LA PORTE - ET LES COUPS DE MARTEAU
DES BLANCS SI DOUX DES PLUMES ET DES SOIES DU
PLAT DE COQUILLAGES DES FLEURS ET DES CRIS
ÉTENDUS SUR LES CORDES DES BOUCHES OUVERTES
VOLANT AUX FENETRES PENDUES AUX RAMEAUX
TORDUS DES TULIPES TEINTES DU VERT ET DU ROUGE

7

MORDUS AUX ANGLES DU VERT BOUTEILLE DU
VASE TREMPANT SES COUTEAUX BIEN EFFILÉS
DANS LE MERCURE DE LA SAUCE QUI MIJOTE
DANS LA PAUME DES MAINS DES LAINES
DU TAPIS CHANTANT SUR LES FEUILLES
BRUTALEMENT SERRÉES EN FOULE SERRÉE
AUX QUATRE COINS DU MUR PEINT A LA CHAUX
ET DÉCHIRÉ SI RAGEUSEMENT SUR SA ROBE
PARFUMÉE DE SON ENCENS INVOLONTAIRE
L'ACCUSE LE POUSSE AUX AVEUX LE TORTURE
LE CHÂTRE ET LE JETTE NU LU SUR LE CIEL
DERRIERE LES NUAGES ACIDULÉS ET LES
OIGNONS DES ROSES FANÉES DES CLOUS
ENFONCÉS SUR LE DOS DES DIVERS QUATRE
MURS DE LA CHAMBRE IMPOSÉE
DE TOUTE PIÈCE ET COLLÉE SUR L'
AIR DE CETTE MUSIQUE QUI PLEUT
INFINIMENT PLUS AGRÉABLEMENT
MÊLÉE AUX COULEURS DU BOUQUET PAR
SES CHEVEUX DÉFAITS ET SES RIRES QUE
PAR SES SAUTS SES CRISES DE NERFS ET SES
LARMES SON SANG QUI COULE GOUTTE À GOUTTE
ET LES GRELOTS DE SES PAILLETES AGITÉES
IGNIFUGENT LES BRINS DE PAILLE DU RIDEAU
QUI DORT DEVANT LA COULEUR CERISE QUI BAIGNE

8

155

180. POEMS AND LITHOGRAPHS

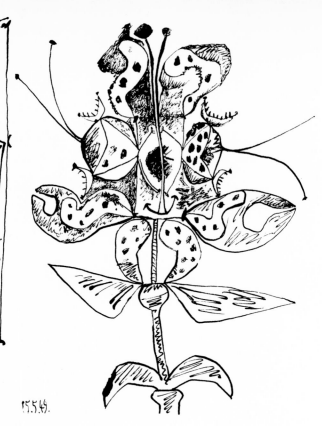

AU BOUT DE SES ONGLES LE MIEL QUI SUINTE
DU PAPIER BLANC QUI S'AGITE ENTRE LES DOITS
DE L'OMBRE ET LA LUMIERE SERRES ETROITEMENT
MOURANT DE PEUR DANS LE COIN LE PLUS MISERABLE
I.5.41. LA FENETRE GRIFFE LA MANTILLE SES CRIS
ECRITS SUR L'ARDOISE À LA CRAIE MONSIEUR MON-
SIEUR VENEZ VENEZ VITE DE SUITE JE DOIS AVANT
RE MIDI FESSER LES FESSES A LA CHAMBRIERE MON.
SIEUR MONSIEUR TOUT EST PRÊT LA CHAMBRE EST
MISE LA TABLE EST PAR DESSUS TOUTE PRÊTE LES
ENFANTS SONT DEJA REVENUS DE L'ECOLE ET
MADAME EST DEJA VIDE DE TOUT SON TRALALA
ET GLACÉE DANS SA ROBE LE TYPE D'A COTÉ L'AIME
CE MATIN ET LA TROUVE RAVISSANTE MONSIEUR
VENEZ MONTEZ VITE C'EST L'HEURE DE SE COUCHER
DE DETACHER LES AILES SI LOURDES DES PIEDS IL
FAIT NOIR ET CE N'EST PAS PRUDENT DE VOUS
LAISSER ALLER TROP LOIN DU PORT EMPORTE PAR
DES VELOURS DES BRIQUES ACCROCHÉES AU BALCON
DES TORCHES ALLUMÉES IL EST IRRESISTIBLEMENT
TROP TARD LA PEAU SE DETACHANT DE LA GRAPPE
DE RAISIN DU CHEVAL VERT DU LINGE L'ENVELOPPANT
RONGE LA LANGUE QUI PEND À SON OEIL EN AVALANT
LA BAVE DES FLAMMES QUI S'AGITENT À L'INTERIEUR
DU VASE PLEIN DE LAIT — LES QUATRE PATTES
DE LA TABLE TREMPENT DANS LA GLACE FONDUE
DE L'ARMOIRE ET S'Y REGARDENT — LA MAIN

9

156

180. POEMS AND LITHOGRAPHS

DE LA PORTE APPUYÉE SUR LE BRAS DU FAUTEUIL
SOUTENU PAR LES PERLES DES RIDEAUX ET LES
VELOURS AMÉTHYSTE DE LA PERSIENNE BRÛLANTE
DES CLOCHES QUI SE RÉVEILLENT HURLENT ET
CAUTÉRISENT LES PLAIES DU SOLEIL SAUPOUDRANT
D'OISEAUX LE COTON DES ROCHERS ET LE LIENT
AUX VAGUES D'ÉCUME DU BOIS DE LA CHARPENTE
SOUTENANT COURAGEUSEMENT LE POIDS DES
COLONNES DE MARBRE - LE FRUIT OUVRE SES
PORTES À TOUT VENANT SES AIGUILLES SE
DÉPLAÇANT AVEC UNE LENTEUR INCONCEVABLE
AU MILIEU DE LA POÊLE OU SAUTENT LES
PATATES DES AILES DE PAPILLON QUI FRIENT
LES ÂMES DANS LE SANG DU BOUDIN GRILLÉ
AU MILIEU DES OIGNONS ET DE LA GUEULE DE
LOUP DU DRAP MARQUÉ À LA GORGE DU LARGE
GALON D'ARGENT DE L'INITIALE PAIN TREMPÉ
DANS L'URINE LA MOUSSE DE BIÈRE MOUILLANT
L'ÉPAULE DES PORTEURS DES CAYES BONDÉES
DE FLEURS ET D'OR QU'EN LANGAGE CLAIR
ET DIT COMME ON DIT COURRAMMENT LES CHOSES
SANS CHERCHER NI MIDI NI QUATORZE HEURES
SIMPLEMENT EN BONS CHIFFRES ET DIEU COMPTÉS
FONT LES UNS SANS LES AUTRES EN GROS PLUS
QUE LA SOMME PREUVE EN PLUS DES FRAIS
PAYÉS DEJÀ POUR AMENDES PLUS PLUS
OU MOINS HONORABLES COMMISSIONS

10

16.5.49. II

PREUVES À L'APPUI CHARGES CHAGRINS
ET LOYERS DE TRANQUILITÉ MAIS LA SOMME
EN DÉTAIL LE PRIX ET LES RENTES LA FORTUNE
LE BONHEUR ET LES CARESSES IMAGINÉES
OU RÉELLES LES RISQUES LES LAMPIONS
ALLUMÉS LE JOUR LES GIRANDOLLES MISES
À PART LES LONGUES COURSES DE LÉVRIERS
D'UNE ÉTOILE À UNE AUTRE ÉTOILE LE DRESSAGE
DES MEUTES SA VIE LA VIE CHAUDS LES MARRONS
REMONTONS À PIEDS JOINTS LA LONGUE LISTE
UN BAQUET PLEIN D'OLIVES NOIRES UN BAQUET
PLEIN D'OLIVES VERTES DEUX LITRES D'HUILE
UN FAUTEUIL EN VELOURS OLIVE UN TAPIS
USAGÉ UNE ARMOIRE UN BAHUT QUELQUES
CHAISES UNE PAIRE DE SANDALES DEUX SABOTS
UN LIT DE CAMP UNE ÉCRITOIRE UNE BAIGNOIRE
DEUX CUVETTES QUATRE TAIES D'OREILLER
AU FOND D'UNE CASSEROLE UN RESTANT DE
COMPOTE DE POMMES ET D'ORANGES UNE
BOÎTE DE RADIS TROIS COUTEAUX UNE FLUTTE
ET DIVERS AUTRES INSTRUMENTS DE
MUSIQUE - AU PIGEONNIER DEUX CENTS
PAIRES DE PIGEONS DES SOURIS ET DES

11

RATS DE LA PAILLE DE LA FIENTE
POUR UNE VALEUR DE MILLE OU DEUX MILLE
CINQ CENT FRANCS - DANS UN SAC À CÔTÉ
DE LA FENÊTRE DE SORTIE DANS
DEUX CAISSES DES GRAINES POUR
SIX MOIS - DANS LA CUISINE LES TROIS FEUX
DES FOURNEAUX LA LAMPE PLEINE DE
PÉTROLE UN PAQUET DE BOUGIES UNE
CORBEILLE EN OSIER PLEINE DE CHARBON
DE BOIS UN PAQUET D'ALLUMETTES UN GRAND POT
EN TERRE PLEIN DE BEURRE FONDU - DU BEURRE
FRAIS DANS UNE ASSIETTE - QUELQUES POMMES DE
TERRE SOUS L'ÉVIER ET QUELQUES POIREAUX
ET OIGNONS - LE BRAS DE FEMME QUI COUPE
EN DEUX LA FENÊTRE VERTE DES FEUILLES
BOURGEONNANTES DU CARRÉ DE MOUCHOIR
DU PAYSAGE QUI CASSE LA GLACE TIÈDE DU
TROU QUI ÉTERNUE LA PETITE FENÊTRE
ACCROCHÉE SUR L'AUTRE - LA SAIGNÉE DU SOLEIL
INFECTANT LA BLESSURE FAITE À L'HEURE
JUSTE DE LA GRASSE MATINÉE APPORTÉE TOUTE
CHAUDE SUR LE MUR DANSANT DU SOL SUR LES
TROIS QUARTS DE LA PIÈCE LA SUR LES
RÉVOLTE AU COEUR DU MORCEAU DE BUFFET
ÉCLAIRÉ GROSSIÈREMENT DU COUDE PAR LA
GIFLE DE LA PORTE OUVERTE BRUSQUEMENT

12

157

180. POEMS AND LITHOGRAPHS

UNE MARE DE CRÈME INONDANT LES SABOTS DES PERSONNAGES
ASSIS ENTRE LES MEUBLES INFESTÉS PAR L'OMBRE
LA FIGURE DE LA NAPPE INONDÉE DE SUEUR CHIANT SES
TRIPES LE BLANC COUVRANT LA ROBE DE CHAUX DU MUR
DU ROSE MORDORÉ SI PÂLE DE LA ROSE ODORANTE DANS
LE DANS LE VERRE. LA COULEUR CIGARE ÉTEINT
ENVELOPPANT LE COIN D'OMBRE ENFONCÉ COMME UN
CLOU DERRIÈRE LA PORTE DE SON ODEUR CRISSANT
LES POILS SOLAIRES AUTOUR DE LA FAUX MOISSONNEUSE
QUI LA BERCE DANS SON SOMMEIL SOMMEIL ET RÉGULARISE
SES PLEURS ET LES RIRES AUX CHIFFRES COLORÉS DES
PUCEAUX DES PLUMES PLANTÉES AU PLAFOND
REFLÉTANT LA MARE PLEINE DES CRIS DES CANARDS
ET DU CUIVRE DU FILET CUEILLI AUX HARPES DES
ROSEAUX DES MACHINES À COUDRE ET À LIRE
LES LIGNES DE LA MAIN POSÉE SUR LE GENOU
DROIT DU CADRE DE LA PORTE TENUE ENTRE-
OUVERTE PAR LE SABRE DE L'ARC EN CIEL
INTRODUISANT SON NEZ 3 Mai 41 LE TIRANT

13

D'ENTRE SES DENTS SA PIPE - LE II ASSIS PAR TERRE
ENVELOPPÉ DE CENDRES - UNE FEMME NUE
DÉTACHANT DE SON CORPS SA CHAIR - DEUX ENFANTS
JOUANT DANS L'EAU D'UN RUISSEAU COULANT LE
LONG DU MUR COUPÉ PAR LE COUP DE HACHE DU
NOIR DESCENDU DU SOLEIL DÉTACHÉ DE LA PAGE
ÉCRITE - MILLE OISEAUX MILLE CINQ CENT
VINGT ET QUATRE SOURIS. LE TRAIT DE TIRE
LIGNE DE LA FLÈCHE TRAVERSANT LE CIEL
COUVERT D'HIRONDELLES POSÉ DESSUS, L'ARC DU
PONT - L'ARC DE LA PORTE D'ENTRÉE - L'ARC
D'UNE GRANDE FENÊTRE À GAUCHE ET LES DIX
AUTRES DU CÔTÉ DROIT - LES PLANTES AROMA-
TIQUES QUI POUSSENT SUR LES DOS DU TOIT
CACHE PAR LES ÉCHAFAUDAGES DE LA TOUR - LA
SŒUR PEIGNANT LES CHEVEUX DE LA ROUE
DU MOULIN FAISANT JEU DE PATIENCE
AVEC LES ROUES DU CHARRIOT PLEIN DE
FOIN - LES ÉNORMES AMPHORES ÉTENDUES
SUR LE SABLE - LE VIN RÉPANDU SUR
LES NAPPES RECOUVRANT LES PLIS DU

14

13.5.49.

13.5.49. 49

CORSAGE COUPANT LE PAIN MIS VOLONTAIREMENT
DROIT SUR LE MATELAS CREUX DU SIFFLET INONDÉ
DU METAL FONDU DES ABEILLES LA CHOUTE HERI-
SSÉE DE CLOUS ET D'EPINGLES
    L'I REMET SA PIPE DANS LA POCHE DE SA
BOUCHE SE MOUCHE SCANDALEUSEMENT
ET ROTE LE II ÉTENDU PAR TERRE
RONFLE ENDORMI. LES ENFANTS
REVENUS SUR L'HERBE SECHANT LEURS
HABITS A L'OMBRE · GOUTE APRÉS GOUTE
LES PIERRES SE GONFLENT ET
VOMISSENT SUR LE MORCEAU DE
MER QU'ON APERÇOIT CACHÉ
DERRIERE LES CHANTS ET LES

15

MUSIQUES DES LILAS POSÉS SUR LES
MEUBLES LA CLOCHE FRAPPE CONTRE
LES NUAGES QUI S'OUVRENT COMME UNE
FLEUR À LA PORTE ARRONDIE PAR LA
VOIX DU SOLEIL QUI DECHARGE LA PATÉE
D'OS ET D'ARÊTES DE SES GRANDS MANTEAUX
ET ROBES D'APPARAT · LES MILLE
QUATRE CENT FRANCS DONNÉS À L'AMI
VENU CE MATIN FLEURISSENT DEJÁ
MÛRS ENTRE LES DRAPS – VENEZ VOIR
LES ENFANTS LES EMPREINTES LAISSÉES
SUR LA FARINE QUI RECOUVRE LA ROBE
BLEUE DE MARIÉE QUI BRULE SUR
LE FEU LA CHEMISE DE DENTELLES
NOIRE LES BAS ET LES BIJOUX
REGORGENT DU FESTIN DE SON CORPS
ET L'ANIMENT DES VOLUBILIS DE
SES GRÂCES ET ALLONGEANT SA
JAMBE JUSQUE AU BOUT DE SON PIED

16

159

180. POEMS AND LITHOGRAPHS

D'UN GRAND COUP DE BOTTE DANS LES CÔTES
RÉVEILLANT LE II - DEUX TU ES UN COCHON
UN PERDU POUR UN ENFANT TROUVÉ UN MORT
UNE HIRONDELLE UNE SAVATE UN CHAMEAU
UN TIROIR DE COMMODE UN CONCOMBRE
UNE TOMATE VEUX TU ME DIRE L'HEURE ET
L'HEURE QU'IL ME FAUT ET PAS UNE AUTRE
UNE HEURE CLAIRE LIMPIDE TRANSPARENTE
ET FRAICHE GLACÉE SORTANT TOUTE SECHE
DE LA SOURCE METS TOI DEBOUT DÉBROUILLE
TES ABATTIS DANSE ET FAIS MOI RIRE 13.V.41
CHASUBLE DE SANG JETÉE SUR LES ÉPAULES
NUES DU BLÉ VERT FRISSONNANT ENTRE
LES DRAPS MOUILLÉS ORCHESTRE SYM-
PHONIQUE DES CHAIRS DÉCHIQUETÉES
PENDUES AUX ARBRES EN FLEURS

17

DU MUR PEINT D'OCRE
AGITANT SES GRANDES AILES VERT
POMME ET BLANC MAUVE SE DÉCHIRANT
LE BEC CONTRE LES VITRES ACHITECTURE
DU SUIF FIXÉ SUR LES VAGUES DE PARFUMS
DE TERRE DE MUSIQUE ET D'OISEAUX CABAS PLEIN
DE PROVISIONS ENTOURÉES DES ROSES GRIM-
PANTES PIQUÉES EN ESSAIM D'ABEILLES ● DANS
LES CHEVEUX DEFAITS DU PAYSAGE ÉTENDU
AU SOLEIL LES QUATRE PATTES DE LA MON-
TAGNE DE RIZ DES ROCHERS POSÉS SUR LES
PIERRES ENFONCÉES DANS LA BOUE
DU CIEL ~~FLEURS~~ JUSQU'AUX CHEVILLES
LA ~~TERRE~~ LANGUE PENDANTE DE LA
CHARRUE COLLÉE AUX LABOURS SUANT
LE PLOMB DU POIDS DE L'EFFORT COMMIS
AU CENTRE DU BOUQUET TORDU PAR LES
CHAINES DES DENTS DES FLEURS SURPRI-
SES AU MILIEU DE LA PEAU RUGUEUSE DE
~~LEUR~~ LEURS YEUX FIXÉS D'EN HAUT

18

160

180. POEMS AND LITHOGRAPHS

EN BAS DE LA ROBE SES PLIS CASSÉS SES DECHIRURES
L'USURE DE L'ETOFFE COUVERTE DE TACHES LES MILLE
ET UN ACROCS SA SALETÉ LA VERMINE LES ARCS DORES
DES PIÈRRES FAISANT LA ROUE ET LES FENETRES
FERMÉES AU LOIN SUR LES MAISONS INCRUSTÉES
AU SABLE FIN DES ARBRES DE LA FORET ET
LES BAILLEMENTS DES PLUMES BLANCHES
ENVOLÉES DU VERRE D'EAU. LES GRANDS CIER-
GES ALLUMÉS DES GROSSES BARQUES ATTENDANT
LE COU LEVÉ LES GOUTTES DE PLUIE DU FLAGEOLET
QUI SOUFFLE MIS AU FRAIS LES OLIVES VERTES DES
DOIGTS LE POT DE ROMARIN COU LEVÉ LES
GRANDS CIERGES ALLUMÉS DES GROSSES BARQUES
COUCHÉES AU BORD DU PUIT ECOUTENT LE PARFUM
DE LA PLUIE QUI SOUFFLE DANS LA FLUTE LES
DOIGTS DES OLIVES VERTES IKKH LA FÊTE
COMMENÇA BIEN PLUS TARD VERS CINQ HEURES
LES ENFANTS DEJÀ COUCHÉS LES BONNES AYANT
MIS LEURS ROBES DE SOIRÉE ET PEIGNÉ LEURS
TRESSES. VETUES DE BLANC D'OEUF LEURS
MEMBRES BAGUÉS DE FEUILLES RIANT COMME DES
BÊTES FRISÈRENT LEURS GESTES ET LEURS GRACES
AUX BULLES DE SAVON QUI S'ENVOLAIENT

19

DES GLACES DES FLECHES DE SOIE QUI
PENDAIENT DE LEURS DANSES ET LES CRIS DES
CLOUS PLANTÉS SUR LEURS CORPS A L'AVEUGLETE
PAR LES TACHES DE FEU DE L'EVIER CONTRAINT
DEMESUREMENT L'ANGOISSE SUSPENDUE AUX
ANGLES DU TAPIS D'ORIENT ROULÉ EN BOULE
SUR LE LIT. L'AMERTUME VERNISSANT LA SOIRÉE
ETENDAIT SA TACHE D'HUILE SUR LES DRAPS-
L'OMBRE QUI SE LEVAIT DU CIEL PLEIN D'ETOILES
COUPAIT EN RONDELLES L'ODEUR DE CANELLE
DU MOINDRE GESTE QUI S'ECHAPPAIT DE LA BOITE DRAPAIENT ORANGES
ET LES SOURCILS JOINTS DES
LEURS NUS DE LA MUSIQUE DEROBEE AUX
COULEURS CACHÉS DERRIERE LES RIDEAUX
PANIER PLEIN DE FILLES TOUTES NUES
BRODÉES D'ARGENT ET D'OR LEURS FRONTS
LEURS SEINS LEURS MAINS LEURS HANCHES
QUAND LA POITRINE DE LA PORTE FRAPPE
DE SES DEUX PIEDS CONTRE LA NUIT
16 septembre 81 A QUATRE HEURES MOINS
LE QUART EXACTEMENT EN PLEIN SOLEIL
L'ENFANT DE L' I ET L' AUTRE EXPOSÉ SUR
LE BORD DE LA FENETRE JOUANT AVEC SES
ONGLES ET SES TACHES D'OMBRE ET DE LUMIERE

20.

180. POEMS AND LITHOGRAPHS

AVX TROMPETTES DES SONNERIES
QVI SE COLLAIENT A SES JOVES MORDOREES
DANS LA GLVE DE PATTES DE MOVCHES
DES BVLLES DE SAVON DE SES CRIS FON-
DANT LA ROBE ROSE A POIS ROVGES AV
BLANC ARDENT DES PASTILLES ODO-
RANTES DE SES CHEVEVX LE SVCRE
FONDV AV FOND DE LA TASSE ET
TOVT LE PAYSAGE INCLVS A L'
INTERIEVR DES POINGS FERMES
DV SOLEIL - LES FRANGES DV
RIDEAV COVVERT DE PVNAISES
LE DECORANT DECORATIVEMENT
DE BLEV ET DE VERT VERONESE
21

SVINTANT METHODIQVEMENT CACHES ET PRVDEMMENT
MIS SOVS CLOCHE LES MVSIQVES LES FEVX DE
BENGALE ET LES PARFVMS DES MAINS VOL
ANTES DES QVELQVES FLEVRS MISES DEBOVT
LEVRS PIQVES PIQVÉES SVR LA PEAV DV PAIN
RECOVVERT D'ENCRE S'AGITANT FOLLEMENT
DANS LE REGLES DV JEV ET LES CEREMONIES
LES CARESSES LES MENACES LES COVPS
TOVTES LEVRS GRIFFES DEHORS IMITANT
TIMIDEMENT L'ORCHESTRE DES DESIRS
ET L'ORPHEON DE DEGOVTS AGITANT DANS
LA SOVPE LEVRS LINGES DECHIRES.
LA MERE VN METRE SOIXANTE-DIX DEVX
BRAS DEVX JAMBES DEVX MAINS DEVX PIEDS
VNE TETE DEVX YEVX DEVX OREILLES VN
NEZ VNE BOVCHE VN ESTOMAC DES
CHEVEVX DES TRIPES DEVX MAMELLES
VN NOMBRIL VN CVL VN CON VINGT DOIGTS
22

180. POEMS AND LITHOGRAPHS

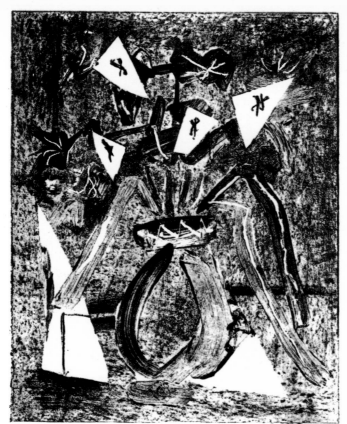

DES POILS... SUR LES JAMBES SUR
LES BRAS SUR LE CUL ET LE CON
DES VEINES DU SANG DES PETS
DE L'URINE DE LA VIANDE DE LA
GRAISSE DES TENDONS ET LE
VENTRE PLEIN D'OS - SA MERE
SA MAMAN ELLE REGARDAIT
L'ENFANT DE L'I ET L'AUTRE
ELLE L'AIMAIT LUI DONNAIT LA
SOUPE DE SE SEINS LE LAVAIT LE
MATIN ET LE SOIR LE PEIGNAIT
ET LUI COUSAIT SES ROBES
ALLAIT AVEC LUI AU CINEMA
AU THEATRE A LA MER
23

ET LUI DONNAIT DES GIFLES
MAMAN MAMAN J'AI FINI
MAMAN DONNE-MOI A BOIRE
MAMAN J'AI SOIF MAMAN J'AI
FAIN MAMAN J'AI SOMMEIL VEUX
-TU QUE JE TE MOUCHE AS-TU
CHAUD AS-TU FROID DODO PIPI
CACA AH QUE LES AILES DU CHE-
VAL SONT LOURDES A PORTER
DIT L'I DEPOSANT LE PAQUET
SUR L'EVIER - NI LA PLUIE
NI LE BEAU TEMPS NI LA
NEIGE ET ENCORE MOINS
LES VIGNES A L'AUTOMNE
24

180. POEMS AND LITHOGRAPHS

ET LES CHAMPS D'
AVOINE ET LE BLE L'ETE ET LE
PRINTEMPS ET L'HIVER REUNIS DANS
UN SEUL BOUQUET LES MILLE DE
MILLIARDS DE LAMPES ALLUMEES
POSEES SUR LA COMMODE.
LE SOPHA CONTRACTE SE HAUSSE
JUSQU'AU PLAFOND LA CHAISE GRINCE
SES CORDES ET LE BOIS VERNIS
DES JUPES DES MARBRES ATTACHES
AUX RIDEAUX DESCENDENT LENTEMENT
LES MARCHES L'HORLOGE COUVRE
SA BOUCHE SUR LA VITRE ET UDILE
LA PLAQUE DE L'HEURE QUI

25

RESPIRE ENCORE DERRIERE LE
RIDEAU DE PLUMES. LE TAPIS MIS
EN BOULE RONRONNE A L'OREILLE DE LA
PORTE DECLOUEE ET MISE AU MILIEU
DE LA CUISINE ELLE SAIGNE BLANCHE COMME
LA CIRE FAITE PAR DES LUNAIRES ABEILLES
LA GRAISSE QUI ENVELOPPE SA ROBE DE LIN
LA SOUTIENT DE SES JASMINS ET L'ENCENS
LA LONGUE TRAINE DU COUTEAU PARTAGE
LA LUMIERE EN DEUX ET LA SEPARE AVEC
SES GRIFFES DU PAPIER COLLANT QUI
LA PRESSE.
LA NUIT QUI SE DETACHE DU MANTEAU
HERBORISE SA PUANTEUR SUR LE LIVRE
OUVERT DE LA FENETRE - UNE LOURDE
EAU DE MELISSE VOLE ENCHAINEE
DANS LA PIECE.

26

164

180. POEMS AND LITHOGRAPHS

181. THE POETRY OF
UNKNOWN WORDS

PICASSO'S UNKNOWN LETTERS

Paris June 1949. Format 3-1/4" x 4-3/4" (8 x 12 cm).
Pen hand-writing on litho paper transferred to stone.

POET'S LITHO

Paris June 1949. Format 7-1/2" x 10-1/4" (19 x 26 cm).
Pen manuscript text on litho paper transferred to stone.

182. VENUS AND LOVE (after Cranach). 1st variation.

Picasso composed these two lithographs for the book
"Poésie de mots inconnus"
published by Iliazd, Paris 1950.
This volume is composed of poems of different authors,
Albert Birot, Artaud, Audiberti, Bull, etc.
illustrated with lithographs and etchings
by Arp, Braque, Chagall, Dominguez, etc.
The justification indicates :
157 copies on "Isle de France" hand made paper:
10 copies on India paper, 3 on wove paper.

182. VENUS AND LOVE (after Cranach) 1st variation.

May 25th, 1949. Format 12-3/4" x 25-1/2" (32,5 x 64,5 cm).
Crayon composition on litho paper, transferred to stone.
The drawing of a head can be seen in the lower part of the plate.
Picasso has turned over the sheet and has begun
his work again without bothering about this first start.
5 artist reserved proofs.
50 numbered and signed proofs.

1st state

183. VENUS AND LOVE (after Cranach). 2nd variation.

2nd state

183. VENUS AND LOVE (after Cranach) 2nd variation.

1st state. May 25th, 1949.
Format 13-3/4" x 25-1/2" (35 x 64,5 cm).
Composition with pen and wash drawing on litho paper
transferred to zinc. 5 artist reserved proofs.
2nd state. May 30th, 1949.
Format 19-3/4" x 26-3/4" (50 x 68 cm).
Re-working of the plate; scrapings with glass paper
and new larger drawing with brush and pen.
5 artist reserved proofs. 50 numbered and signed proofs.
This state is known as:
"Venus and love on black background".

184. VENUS AND LOVE (after Cranach). 3rd variation.

167

184. VENUS AND LOVE (after Cranach) 3rd variation.

May 25th, 1949. Format 15" x 30" (38 x 76 cm).
Pen drawing and wash drawing with litho ink
on transfer paper. Transfer to stone.
5 artist reserved proofs.
50 numbered and signed proofs.
At this point Picasso executes some drawings
and etchings on the same theme.

185. TROPICAL PLANTS

May 15th, 1949. Format 18-1/2" x 24-1/2" (47 x 62 cm).
Pen composition on transfer paper
transferred to stone. 5 artist reserved proofs.
50 numbered and signed proofs.

*Living in the Midi during 1950, the artist
was occupied with painting, sculpture and
ceramics and produced no lithographs for
almost a year. It was only at the insistence
of his friends that Picasso took up his
lithographic crayon again.
The printing of the 2nd volume
of the four-volume edition of
"Picasso Lithographs"
was nearing completion.
I went to see Picasso at Vallauris to show
him the final proofs and to obtain
the cover lithograph.
"You shall have it tomorrow, Mourlot."
And indeed, the next day, he shut himself
up in his workshop and set to work.
Picasso had neither a greasy litho crayon
nor a brush, but he found a way round
this difficulty. He put some water into
the litho ink container and with
his finger thinned the solidified ink.
In this way he completed
the extraordinarily life-like portraits
of his children Claude and Paloma.
As it was still early in the day he still had time
to produce the nine lithos for the book :
"De Mémoire d'homme" that Tristan Tzara
had been asking him for for several months,*
168 *using the same technique.*

186. PALOMA AND CLAUDE

186. PALOMA AND CLAUDE

Vallauris, April 16th, 1950. Composition format 12-1/2" x 20-1/2" (32 x 52 cm).
In this composition the artist applied the litho ink, thinned as required,
with his fingers. Transfer to stone.
Printing of 2,000 proofs for the cover impression of vol. II
of the four volume edition of "Picasso lithographs". André Sauret, Publisher.
5 artist reserved proofs with date indicated under the composition.

187. WITHIN LIVING MEMORY

187. WITHIN LIVING MEMORY

Vallauris, April 16th, 1950.
Format of the volume 10" x 12-3/4" (25 x 32.5 cm).
First edition of the poem "De mémoire d'homme" of Tristan Tzara,
illustrated with nine Pablo Picasso original lithographs.
30 proofs on Van Gelder Dutch paper plus a follow up
on Japan paper, numbered from 1 to 30.
300 copies on Arches wove paper numbered from 31 to 330.
20 copies not for sale on Alfa moss paper marked
in Roman figures. Bordas Publisher, 1950.
Stones polished out after printing.

188. YOUTH

1st state

2nd state

170

188. YOUTH

1st state.   Vallauris, May 1950.
Format 19-3/4" x 25-1/2" (50 x 65 cm).
Picasso is urged to produce a poster for
a franco-italian friendship day in Nice.
Here is the composition executed with litho
crayon, brush and gouache on transfer paper.
Transfer to zinc. The gouache, thinned down
with water at the time of transfer,
resulted in a failure of the inking.
5 artist reserved proofs.

2nd state.   June 9th, 1950.
Format 19-3/4" x 25-1/2" (50 x 65 cm).
Re-working of zinc with litho crayon and ink.
Printing of original zinc.   5 artist reserved proofs.
50 numbered and signed proofs.
1,000 copies of the poster are printed by
transfer to stone of the original zinc with the text:
"Rencontre internationale de Nice 13-20 août 1950"
(Internat. Meeting at Nice). 13th-20th August, 1950,
format 31-1/2" x 47-1/4" (80 x 120 cm).
A version of the poster is photographically
printed, format 15-3/4" x 23-1/2" (40 x 60 cm),
the image being reduced.

189. FLOWERS IN A VASE

189. FLOWERS IN A VASE

Vallauris, May 5th, 1950. Format 9-1/2" x 6-1/4" (24,5 x 16 cm).
Litho crayon drawing on transfer paper transferred to stone for the
"Poteries-Art et Technique" exhibition at Vallauris, July-September 1950.
Poster printed in the format 19" x 25-1/2" (48 x 65 cm). 350 copies.
The litho, folded in two, serves also as a frontispiece for the
de luxe copies of the exhibition catalogue.
An additional 100 copies were printed with wording omitted with margins on Arches
thin wove paper (19" x 12-3/4"—48 x 65 cm) of which the artist signed
a few copies for the benefit of the Vallauris Museum.

190. DOVE IN FLIGHT, BLACK BACKGROUND

191. THE FLYING DOVE

172

190. DOVE IN FLIHGT, BLACK BACKGROUND

Vallauris, July 9th, 1950.
Format 19-1/2" x 25-1/2" (49,5 x 64,5 cm).
A set of 4 "Dove in flight" lithos produced for possible use as a poster for the 11th peace congress to be held in London in November 1950. This first project, litho crayon flat scumbled and gouache on litho paper, is abandoned.
More than two years later Picasso rediscovers
this composition rolled up in a corner of the Vallauris studio and sends it to me. The transfer, and inking
are successful and prints are made.
5 artist reserved proofs. 50 numbered and signed proofs.

191. THE FLYING DOVE

Vallauris, July 9th, 1950.
Format 21-1/4" x 23-1/2" (54 x 60 cm).
Composition executed on zinc with a crayon
and lithographic ink stick.
This plate, like plate No. 192, was printed in 1955.
5 artist reserved proofs.
50 numbered and signed proofs.

192. THE FLIGHT OF THE DOVE

193. DOVE IN FLIGHT

192. THE FLIGHT OF THE DOVE

Vallauris, July 9th, 1950.
Format 21-1/2″ x 28″ (54,5 x 71 cm).
Composition on zinc, same process as for
the preceding number. Printed in 1955.
5 artist reserved proofs.
50 numbered and signed proofs.

193. DOVE IN FLIGHT

Vallauris, July 9th, 1950. Format 21-3/4″ x 27-1/2″ (55 x 70 cm).
Composition on zinc, same process as for the two preceding projects.
Note the use of an unmoistened litho ink stick
which produces the firm lines of this drawing. Printing from the original zinc.
5 artist reserved proofs. 50 numbered and signed proofs.
This plate is the one selected for the poster;
the original zinc is transferred to stone and printed.
The dove is pulled on a light buff background with the text below.
Format of the poster: 31-1/2″ x 47-1/4″ (80 x 120 cm).
A reduction of this poster to 15-3/4″ x 23-1/2″ (40 x 60 cm).
is photographically printed.

194. HEADS AND STONE

194. HEADS AND STONE

Paris, November 26th, 1950.
Format 19″ x 25″ (48 x 63 cm).
Back in Paris. Drawing made on Arches paper,
but with a litho crayon and some gouache:
why not try to transfer it ?
It is a great success and Picasso is satisfied
with the result and also pleased to get his drawing back
nearly undamaged. (It was, however, slightly damaged.)
5 artist reserved proofs.
50 numbered and signed proofs.

1st state

2nd state

195. FRANÇOISE ON GREY BACKGROUND

195. FRANÇOISE ON GREY BACKGROUND

1st state. Paris, November 5th, 1950.
Format 19″ x 25″ (48 x 63 cm).
Portrait executed on zinc with litho crayon
and wash drawing. 5 artist reserved proofs.
2nd state. November 19th, 1950.
Format 19″ x 25″ (48 x 63 cm).
Re-working of zinc with litho crayon:
printing on Ingres Canson sized blue-grey paper
and set on Arches wove paper,
format 22″ x 30″ (56 x 76 cm). 5 artist reserved proofs.
50 numbered and signed proofs.

196. THE PIKE

196. THE PIKE

November 26th, 1950.
Format 19" x 25-1/4" (48 x 64 cm).
Composition with litho crayon on transfer paper
transferred to stone.
5 artist reserved proofs.
50 numbered and signed proofs.

2nd state of black

197. WOMAN AT THE MIRROR

2nd state of the complete plate

1st state

197. WOMAN AT THE MIRROR

1st state.   Paris, November 16th, 1950.
Format 12-3/4"x19-3/4" (32,5 x 50 cm).
Black: Composition on litho paper
transferred to zinc with pen.
Yellow ochre: wash drawing made
with brush on transparent litho paper.
5 artist reserved proofs.

2nd state of black: December 10th, 1950.
Erasing with glass paper,
re-worked with pen
5 artist reserved proofs.
2nd state of the complete plate:
No change on the black zinc.
The yellow plate has been rubbed
with glass paper after some additions.
The yellow is printed with red ochre.
5 artist reserved proofs.

3rd state of black

3rd state of the second colour

4th state

178

197. WOMAN AT THE MIRROR

3rd state of black: December 15th, 1950.
Format 14-1/2" x 19-1/4" (37 x 49 cm).
Erasures and changes in the drawing.
4th state. Paris, November 5th, 1953.
Format 15-3/4" x 20-1/2" (40 x 52 cm).
The black zinc is re-worked, particularly
the left arm, the face and the small vase.
The half-tints, a little more
reinforced than in the 3rd state, are scraped in parts
which slightly tones up the whole.
A second colour, bistre, is produced
with litho crayon. 11/11/53.
5 artist reserved proofs. Zincs preserved.

3rd state of the second colour.
December 15th, 1950.
Format 12-1/2" x 19-1/4" (32 x 49 cm).
This zinc already printed in yellow ochre then in red
is re-worked and re-drawn.
The 2nd colour is abandoned.
5 black proofs for the artist.
Zinc preserved.

THE KNIGHTS

198. LINE-DRAWN LITTLE KNIGHT

199. PAGES' GAMES

200. THE KNIGHT AND THE PAGE

198. LINE-DRAWN LITTLE KNIGHT

Paris, January 12th, 1951. Format 8-1/4"x9-1/2" (21 x 24,5 cm).
At my request, Picasso makes a trial stone-engraving.
But the stone is not well prepared and the artist
is not very satisfied with the result obtained.
5 artist reserved proofs. Stone preserved.

199. PAGES' GAMES

Vallauris, February 19th, 1951. Format 12-1/2"x16-3/4" (32 x 42,5 cm).
Picasso suddenly leaves for the south of France but he does not want
to abandon lithography and his Knights and he takes two small stones

with him which he sends back to me a few days later.
Pen and litho crayon composition.
Erasures, all very finely executed.
5 artist reserved proofs. 50 numbered and signed proofs.

200. THE KNIGHT AND THE PAGE

Vallauris, February 17th, 1951.
Format 14-1/2"x10-1/2" (36,5 x 26,5 cm).
Litho crayon, pen, scrapings on stone.
Note the black printed stone edges.
5 artist reserved proofs. 50 numbered and signed proofs.

201. THE DEPARTURE

201. THE DEPARTURE

180

201. THE DEPARTURE

Paris, March 12th, 1951.
Format 13-1/2"x17" (34,5 x 43 cm).
Brush composition on zinc;
this plate is to form the basis
for a colour lithograph.
5 sanguine proofs for the artist.

201. THE DEPARTURE

The same plate is printed in black on a pink background.
5 artist reserved proofs.

201. THE DEPARTURE

201. THE DEPARTURE

201. THE DEPARTURE

Paris, April 2nd, 1951.
Format 14/1/4" x 17-1/4" (36 x 44 cm).
Pen and wash drawing composition
on a reproduction proof on zinc
of the March 12th, plate.
5 artist reserved proofs.

201. THE DEPARTURE

Format 14-1/4" x 17-1/4" (36 x 44 cm).
Proof obtained with the impression of the
March 12th plate in sanguine and of the April 2nd
plate in black and a light grey background.
(same stone as the printing of page 180).
5 artist preserved proofs

201. THE DEPARTURE

201. THE DEPARTURE

182

201. THE DEPARTURE

Paris, May 1st, 1951.
Format 13-3/4" x 17-1/4" (35 x 44 cm).
Clear reproduction proof on a black coated stone.
The artist, therefore, has to engrave to obtain whites.
5 artist reserved proofs.

201. THE DEPARTURE

May 21st, 1951.
Format 13-3/4" x 17-1/4" (35 x 44 cm).
The May 1st stone is re-worked with scraper.
5 artist reserved proofs.

201. THE DEPARTURE

201. THE DEPARTURE

201. THE DEPARTURE

Proof obtained with the impression of the
March 12th zinc in dark ochre;
the May 21st black stone and the ochre background
5 artist reserved proofs.
Stone kept at the workshop, rue des Grands Augustins.

201. THE DEPARTURE

Paris, April 30th, 1951.
Format 22"x17-3/4" (56x45 cm).
In the meantime, Picasso made a new composition
on litho paper for the black.
Reproduction proof on zinc and printing
on a sanguine proof of March 12th.
A single proof, zinc polished out.

201. THE DEPARTURE

201. THE DEPARTURE

184

201. THE DEPARTURE

May 20th, 1951.
Format 22"×17-3/4" (56×45 cm).
New black plate made with ink on zinc.
5 artist reserved proofs.

201. THE DEPARTURE

Final state. Format 26"×22" (66×56 cm).
Proof obtained with the March 12th zinc,
the May 20th zinc, a grey flat and ochre frame.
5 artist reserved proofs.
50 numbered and signed proofs.

203. THE FACE OF PEACE. 2nd version.

202. THE FACE OF PEACE. 1st version.

202. THE FACE OF PEACE. 1st version.

September 10th, 1951.
Format 9-1/2" x 7-1/4" (24,5 x 18,5 cm).
Litho crayon composition on transfer paper
transferred to stone. Bad transfer.
Picasso abandons the stone,
later polished out according to his instructions.
5 artist reserved proofs.

203. THE FACE OF PEACE. 2nd version.

September 29th, 1951.
Format 10-1/4" x 7-1/4" (26 x 18,5 cm).
Composition with litho crayon on transfer paper
transferred to stone. This lithograph served as
a frontispiece to the de luxe edition of the volume
"Le visage de la Paix" by Picasso and Eluard.
Editions Cercle d'Art, Paris 1951.
Format 11" x 8-3/4" (28 x 22,5 cm).
150 copies printed on Johannot pure linen wove
paper numbered in Roman numerals from I to CL.
Stone polished out.

204. POSTER FOR THE HISPANO-AMERICAN EXHIBITION

205

206

204. POSTER FOR
THE HISPANO-AMERICAN EXHIBITION

Litho crayon composition on transfer paper
transferred to stone.
300 copies of the poster printed with ochre background,
format 18-3/4" x 25-1/2" (48 x 65 cm)
100 proofs were printed on register wove paper
signed by the artist for the exhibition.

POSTER FOR THE HISPANO-AMERICAN EXHIBITION

Vallauris, November 4th, 1951. For his spanish friends,
Picasso composed the poster for
the Hispano-American Exhibition; it was published (No. 2
but at that time three possible alternatives were produced
the two litho crayon compositions (Nos. 205 and 206),
not retained, remained in a portfolio at Vallauris.
When I called upon him at Cannes in April 1956
Picasso rediscovered them: transfer.
No. 205. Format 18-1/2" x 14-1/4" (47 x 36 cm).
No. 206. Format 19" x 15-1/4" (48 x 39 cm).
5 proofs of each of these 2 posters for the artist.

207. DON QUIXOTE AND SANCHO PANZA I

208. DON QUIXOTE AND SANCHO PANZA II

209 THE KNIGHT AND THE PAGE

207. DON QUIXOTE AND SANCHO PANZA I

Format 11-1/4" x 12-1/4" (29 x 31 cm).
Litho No. 205 altered and
printed with ochre background.
5 artist reserved proofs. 50 numbered and signed proofs.

208. DON QUIXOTE AND SANCHO PANZA II

Format 13-1/4" x 13-1/4" (34 x 34 cm).
Composition No. 206 is also altered.
5 artist reserved proofs. 50 numbered and signed proofs.

209. THE KNIGHT AND THE PAGE

Vallauris, March 28th, 1951.
Format 18-3/4" x 15-1/2" (48 x 39,5 cm).
Composition with lead pencil executed by Picasso
on a zinc which was brought to him by a Marseilles lithographer.
4 artist reserved proofs.

POSTER FOR THE IIIRD PEACE CONGRESS

210. BOUND HANDS I

211. BOUND HANDS II

Picasso agrees to produce a model
for the poster for the
IIIRD Peace Congress to be held
in Vienna from 12th to
18th December, 1952.
One after the other he rejects
the six following compositions.
Finally he selected an etching -
which is to be photographically
reproduced for this poster in the format
31-1/2" x 47" (80 x 120 cm).

210. BOUND HANDS I

Vallauris, September 25th, 1952.
Format 18" x 24" (46 x 61 cm).
Litho crayon composition on zinc.
5 artist reserved proofs. 50 numbered and signed proofs.

211. BOUND HANDS II

Vallauris, September 25th, 1952.
Format 18" x 23-3/4" (46 x 60,5 cm).
Litho crayon composition on zinc.
5 artist reserved proofs. 50 numbered and signed proofs.

212. BOUND HANDS III

213. BOUND HANDS IV

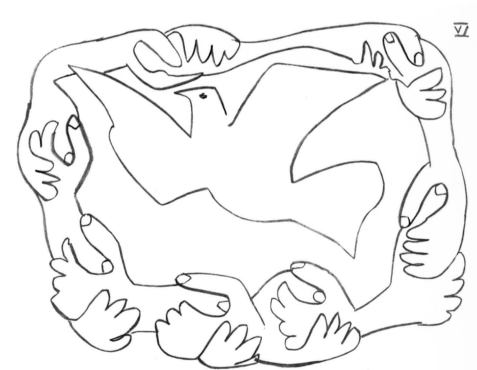

212. BOUND HANDS III

Vallauris, September 25th, 1952.
Format 17-3/4" x 23-1/2" (45 x 60 cm).
Litho crayon composition on zinc.
5 artist reserved proofs.
50 numbered and signed proofs.

213. BOUND HANDS IV

Vallauris, September 25th, 1952.
Format 18" x 23-1/2" (46 x 60 cm).
Litho crayon composition on zinc.
The proof bears the Roman numeral VI
(IV on the reverse side)
although it is the 4th version produced.
5 artist reserved proofs.
50 numbered and signed proofs.

214. FLYING DOVE

214. FLYING DOVE

Vallauris, October 10th, 1952.
Format of the composition
17-3/4" x 24-1/2" (45 x 62 cm).
Litho crayon and gouache drawing on transfer paper
transferred to stone.
5 artist reserved proofs.
Stone polished out.

215. THE RAINBOW DOVE

215. THE RAINBOW DOVE

Vallauris, October 23rd, 1952.
Format 19-3/4" x 25-1/2" (50 x 65 cm).
Litho crayon drawing on transfer paper cut and pasted
on the rainbow background. Transfer to stone.
5 artist reserved proofs.

*Picasso arrived in Paris for a few days and
I asked him to do a portrait of Balzac for the
publisher Sauret, taking him
the necessary equipment for the work in case
he is short of anything.
The following morning Picasso telephoned me
and I called on him at Rue Gay-Lussac.
Picasso handed me 8 litho drawings, in the
required format, made on transfer paper
numbered from I to VIII (Nos. 216 to 223)
as well as 3 large compositions
(Nos 225 to 227).
A few days later, on 7th December, 1952,
he re-worked a crayon litho (No. 224) and also
an etching of the same subject.*

216. FRONTISPIECE FOR "LE PERE GORIOT"

216. FRONTISPIECE FOR "LE PERE GORIOT"

November 25th, 1952.
Format of the book 6-1/4" x 8-3/4" (16 x 22 cm).
Pen drawing on transfer paper transferred to stone.
Grand Prix of the best XIXth Century Novels.
André Sauret, Publisher, 1952.
Run of 300 copies on Arches laid paper,
300 on India Paper and 3,100 copies on wove paper.
This litho, in the set of 8, was marked No. 2 in the margin
which was larger than the format of the book.

217

219

218

220

222

221

193

225. BALZAC

223

224

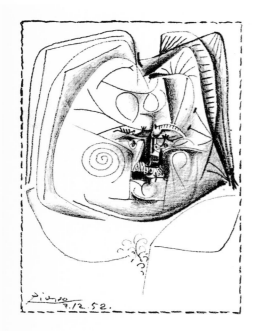

194

225. BALZAC

Paris, November 25th, 1952.
Format 20-1/2" x 26-3/4" (52 x 68 cm).
Litho crayon drawing on transfer paper
transferred to stone.
5 artist reserved proofs.
25 numbered and signed proofs.

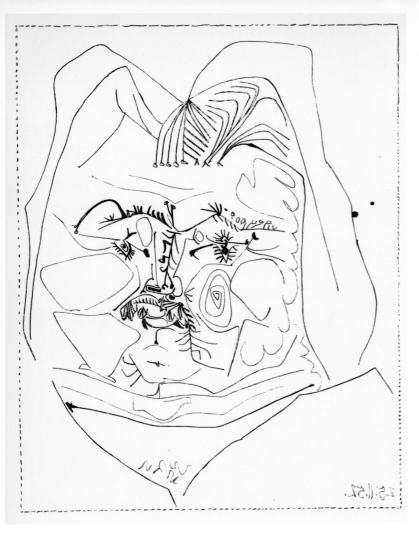

226. BALZAC

227. BALZAC

226. BALZAC

Paris, November 25th, 1952.
Format 20-3/4" x 27-1/2" (53 x 70 cm).
Litho ink composition on transfer paper
transferred to stone.
5 artist reserved proofs.
25 numbered and signed proofs.

227. BALZAC

Paris, November 25th, 1952.
Format 20-1/2" x 27" (52 x 69 cm).
Litho crayon composition on transfer paper
transferred to stone.
5 artist reserved proofs.
25 numbered and signed proofs.

Back in Vallauris for just a few days, Picasso nevertheless continued working on his lithographs. Here are three portraits of the little Paloma as well as three busts of women and a still life with book. In producing these compositions the resists were obtained by the use of lithographic crayon and seccotine (an original process to say the least).

228. PALOMA AND HER DOLL, WHITE BACKGROUND

228. PALOMA AND HER DOLL, WHITE BACKGROUND

Vallauris, December 14th, 1952.
Format 21-1/4" x 28-1/2" (54 x 72 cm).
Litho crayon composition on zinc.
5 artist reserved proofs.
50 numbered and signed proofs.

229. PALOMA AND HER DOLL, BLACK BACKGROUND

230. PALOMA

229. PALOMA AND HER DOLL, BLACK BACKGROUND

Vallauris, December 14th, 1952.
Format 21-3/4" x 27-1/2" (55 x 70 cm).
Litho crayon composition on zinc,
reserve drawings with scraper.
5 artist reserved proofs.
50 numbered and signed proofs.

230. PALOMA

Vallauris, December 24th, 1952.
Format 12-1/2" x 15-3/4" (32 x 40 cm).
Litho crayon composition on zinc.
5 artist reserved proofs.
50 numbered and signed proofs.

232. WOMAN'S HEAD, THREE-QUARTER-FACE

231. THE EMBROIDERED SWEATER

231. THE EMBROIDERED SWEATER

Vallauris, January 3rd, 1953.
Format 13-3/4" x 18" (35 x 46 cm).
Litho crayon composition on zinc;
the whites have been reserved with seccotine.
These reserves made, the artist has scumbled his crayon
to make his drawing. The zinc has probably
been badly grained and an earlier
composition that Picasso's crayon
has re-inked appears here and there.
5 artist reserved proofs.
50 numbered and signed proofs.

232. WOMAN'S HEAD, THREE-QUARTER-FACE

Vallauris, January 4th, 1953.
Format 17-3/4" x 21-1/4" (45 x 54 cm).
Same process as for No. 231.
5 artist reserved proofs.
50 numbered and signed proofs.

233. WOMAN'S HEAD WITH CHIGNON

234. STILL LIFE WITH BOOK

235. THE FAMILY

233. WOMAN'S HEAD WITH CHIGNON

Vallauris, January 4th, 1953.
Format 17" x 25-1/2" (43 x 65 cm).
Same process as for Nos. 231 and 232
5 artist reserved proofs.
50 numbered and signed proofs.

234. STILL LIFE WITH BOOK

Vallauris, January 4th, 1953. Format 11" x 16-1/2" (28 x 42 cm).
Same process as for the preceding numbers.
5 artist reserved proofs. 50 numbered and signed proofs.

235. THE FAMILY

Paris, January 17th, 1953.
Format 11-1/2" x 15-1/2" (29,5 x 39,5 cm).
Composition executed with litho crayon and scraper on a zinc
on which a grain screen had been transferred for quite another use
5 artist reserved proofs. 50 numbered and signed proofs.

236. GARDENS AT VALLAURIS

237. LANDSCAPE AT VALLAURIS

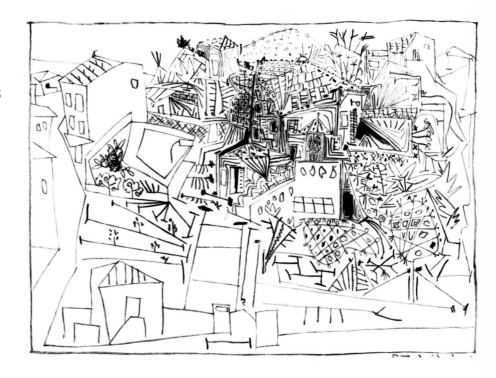

236. GARDENS AT VALLAURIS

Paris, January 15th, 1953.
Format 20" x 25-1/4" (51 x 64 cm).
Litho crayon composition on zinc.
5 artist reserved proofs. 50 numbered and signed proofs.

237. LANDSCAPE AT VALLAURIS

Paris, January 15th, 1953.
Format 20" x 25-1/2" (51 x 65 cm).
Litho crayon composition on zinc.
5 artist reserved proofs. 50 numbered and signed proofs.

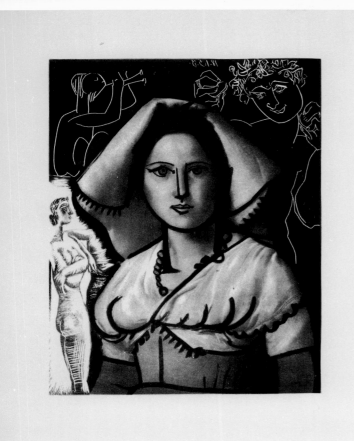

1st state

2nd state

238. THE ITALIAN WOMAN (after Victor Orsel's picture)

Picasso visits the printing works, greets everyone and notices
some zincs lying in a corner of the workshop
waiting to be polished out. He likes one, but it is unusable.
It is a screened photolithography which was used
for the poster printing "La peinture lyonnaise"
at the Tuileries Orangery in November 1948.
Delighted, Picasso takes it away.
The next day he brings back the modified zinc.
1st state. Paris, January 18th, 1953.
Format 13-3/4" x 17-1/2" (35 x 44,5 cm). Wide brush drawing
and engraving in the backgrounds. 5 artist reserved proofs.

2nd state.   January 21st, 1953.
Format 15" x 17-1/2" (38 x 44,5 cm).
The zinc is re-engraved in the background.
A few parts lightly re-worked with brush.
Not printed until 1955.
5 artist reserved proofs.
50 numbered and signed proofs.

239. MOTHER AND CHILDREN

240. GAMES AND READING

202

239. MOTHER AND CHILDREN

Paris, January 20th, 1953.
Format 19" x 29-1/4" (48 x 74 cm).
Wash drawing composition on zinc.
5 artist reserved proofs. 50 numbered and signed proofs.

240. GAMES AND READING

Paris, January 23rd, 24th, 1953. Format 19" x 25" (48 x 63 cm).
Wash drawing and pen composition on zinc.
5 artist reserved proofs. Zinc preserved.

1. HEAD ON BLACK BACKGROUND

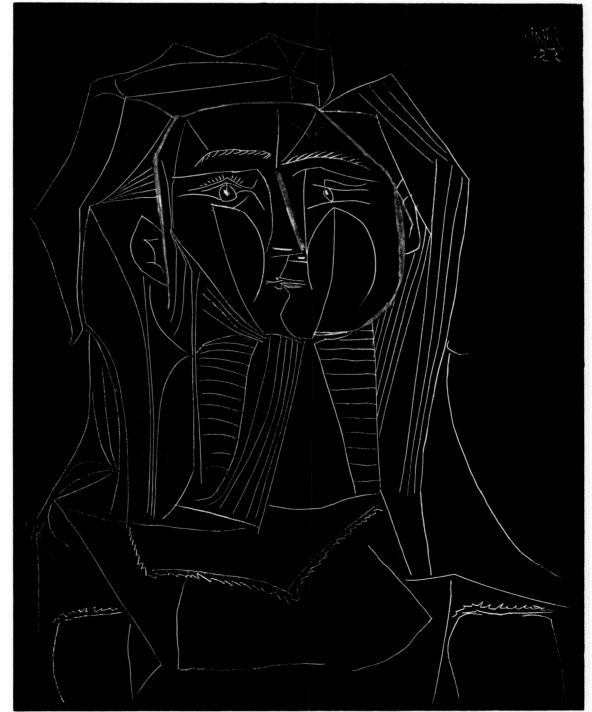

241. HEAD ON BLACK BACKGROUND

May 9th, 1953. Format 21-1/2" x 27-1/4" (54,5 x 69,5 cm).
Engraved composition on zinc intended for etching.
but as the zinc is slightly grained,
this process cannot be used.
Picasso decides to try and have it negative printed
on the lithographic press, with a very good result.
5 artist reserved proofs.
50 numbered and signed proofs.

242. PORTRAIT OF MADAME X

242. PORTRAIT OF MADAME X

November 2nd, 1953. Format 21″ x 30-3/4″ (53 x 78 cm).
Litho crayon on transfer paper transferred to zinc.
5 artist reserved proofs.
Zinc preserved.

243. WOMAN WITH MONKEY

244. RECLINING MODEL

243. WOMAN WITH MONKEY

Vallauris, February 7th, 1954. Format 12-3/4"x10" (32x25 cm).
Litho crayon composition on transfer paper transferred to stone.
At this time Picasso begins a set of remarkable lithographs
after the astonishing series of drawings,
(November 1953 - February 1954) many of which were
reproduced in No. 29-30 of the magazine "Verve".
5 artist reserved proofs.
25 numbered and signed proofs with yellow ochre background.
25 numbered and signed proofs without background.

244. RECLINING MODEL

Vallauris, February 11-12th, 1954.
Format 12"x8-1/4"·(30,5x21 cm).
Litho crayon composition transferred to stone.
5 artist reserved proofs.
25 numbered and signed proofs
with ochre background.
25 numbered and signed proofs without background.

245. WAR AND PEACE

246. DANCES

206

245. WAR AND PEACE

February 10th, 1954.
Format 9-1/2" x 11-3/4" (24 x 30 cm).
Frontispiece for the de luxe copies of the book
"La Guerre et la Paix".
text by Claude Roy.
Editions du Cercle d'Art, 1954.
Run of 100 copies on Arches wove paper,
signed by the Artist.

246. DANCES

Vallauris, February 13th, 1954.
Format 19" x 24-1/2" (48 x 62 cm).
Litho crayon composition on transfer paper
transferred to stone.
5 artist reserved proofs.
50 numbered and signed proofs.

247. BULL AT PLAY

248. THE DANCE OF THE BANDERILLAS

247. BULL AT PLAY

Vallauris, February 14th, 1954.
Format 18-3/4" x 25-1/4" (47,5 x 64 cm).
Litho crayon composition on transfer paper
transferred to stone.
5 artist reserved proofs.
50 numbered and signed copies.

248. THE DANCE OF THE BANDERILLAS

Vallauris, February 14th, 1954.
Format 19" x 25-1/4" (48 x 64 cm).
Same process as the preceding number.
5 artist reserved proofs.
50 numbered and signed proofs.

249. THE TUMBLER'S FAMILY

250. TROUPE OF ACTORS

249. THE TUMBLER'S FAMILY

Vallauris, February 16th, 1954.
Format 19-3/4" x 25-1/4" (50 x 64 cm).
Litho crayon composition on transfer paper.
Transferred to stone. Stone polished out.
5 artist reserved proofs.
50 numbered and signed proofs.

250. TROUPE OF ACTORS

Vallauris, February 17th, 1954.
Format 19-1/4" x 25-1/4" (49 x 64 cm).
Same process as for the preceding number.
Stone polished out.
5 artist reserved proofs.
50 numbered and signed proofs.

251. THE THREE WOMEN AND THE TOREADOR

251. THE THREE WOMEN AND THE TOREADOR

Vallauris, February 17th, 1954.
Format 19-3/4" x 25-1/2" (50 x 65 cm).
Litho crayon composition on litho paper.
Transferred to stone. 5 artist reserved proofs.
50 numbered and signed proofs. Stone polished out.

252. THE REHEARSAL

253. THE TWO MODELS

252. THE REHEARSAL

Vallauris, February 21st, 22nd, 23rd, 24th, 25th, 26th, 1954
Format 19-1/2" x 25-1/2" (49,5 x 65 cm).
Litho crayon composition on transfer paper
transferred to stone. Remarkable composition
on which the artist certainly spent much time.
The transfer was a perfect success; I need hardly say
that a poor transfer would have earned me
no praise. 5 artist reserved proofs.
50 numbered and signed proofs.
Stone polished out.

253. THE TWO MODELS

Vallauris, March 8th, 1954.
Format 19-1/2" x 24-3/4" (49,5 x 63 cm).
Litho crayon composition on transfer paper
transferred to stone. 5 artist reserved proofs.
50 numbered and signed proofs. Stone polished out.

254. FIGURES AND DOVE

255. NUDE POSE

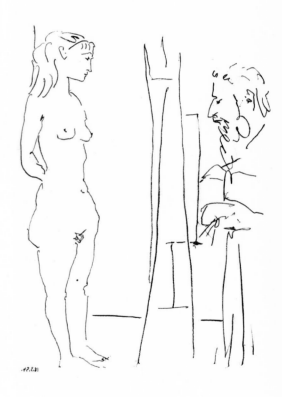

254. FIGURES AND DOVE

Vallauris, March 13th, 1954.
Format 19-5" x 25-1/2" (49,5 x 65 cm).
Same process as the preceding number.
5 artist reserved proofs.
50 numbered and signed proofs.
Stone polished out.

255. NUDE POSE

Vallauris, March 18th, 1954.
Format 15" x 21-1/4" (38 x 54 cm).
Litho crayon composition on transfer paper
transferred to stone.
5 artist reserved proofs.
50 numbered and signed proofs.

256. TWO NUDE MODELS

257. CLOTHED POSE

256. TWO NUDE MODELS

Vallauris, March 18th, 1954.
Format 15" x 22-3/4" (38 x 58 cm).
Same process as the preceding number.
5 artist reserved proofs.
50 numbered and signed proofs.

257. CLOTHED POSE

Vallauris, March 19th and 26th, 1954.
Format 15" x 21-1/2" (38 x 55 cm).
Wash drawing with litho ink composition
executed on zinc.
5 artist reserved proofs.
50 numbered and signed proofs.
Zinc polished out.

258. MODEL AND TWO FIGURES

259. DANCER

258. MODEL AND TWO FIGURES

Vallauris, March 14th, 1954.
Format 19-3/4" x 25-1/2" (50 x 65 cm).
During the same period Picasso composed
a few lithographs in colours by utilizing opaque
and transparent transfer paper.
This one comprises 4 colours: green, blue, red, bistre
Transfer on stones of each different colour.
5 artist reserved proofs.
50 numbered and signed proofs. Stones polished out.

259. DANCER

Vallauris, March 1954.
Format 6-1/4" x 11-1/2" (16 x 29 cm).
Lithograph in 4 colours. Each colour is executed
with litho crayon on transfer paper
transferred to stone.
Frontispiece for Boris Kochno's book "Le Ballet"
Hachette, Publisher, 1954. 1,000 copies.
5 artist reserved proofs. 50 numbered and signed proofs.

260. THE OLD PAINTER'S STUDIO

261. NUDE WITH CHAIR

214

260. THE OLD PAINTER'S STUDIO

Vallauris, March 14th, 1954.
Format 20-1/2"x13" (52x33 cm).
Lithograph in 5 colours. Each of the 5 colours is executed
with litho crayon on transparent transfer paper
and transferred to stone.
Printing is registered on hand press.
5 artist reserved proofs.
50 numbered and signed proofs.

261. NUDE WITH CHAIR

Vallauris, March 18th, 1954.
Format 9-1/2"x6-1/4" (24x16 cm).
Lithograph in 4 colours.
Each colour is executed with litho crayon
on transfer paper and transferred to stone.
5 artist reserved proofs.
50 numbered and signed proofs.

262. THE PAINTER AND HIS MODEL

262 (a). THE PAINTER AND HIS MODEL

262. THE PAINTER AND HIS MODEL

Vallauris, March 25th, 1954.
Format 25-1/4″ x 19-3/4″ (64 x 50 cm).
Lithograph in 5 colours.
Same process as for the preceding compositions.
Before deciding upon this range of colours
Picasso wanted to have these stones pulled
in a general effect of grey.
5 artist reserved proofs.
50 numbered and signed proofs.

262 (a). THE PAINTER AND HIS MODEL

Vallauris, March 25th, 1954.
This lithograph is pulled in grey and black on the
stones of the preceding proof. This range is rejected.
5 artist reserved proofs.
Stones polished out after the final printing.

263. THE LITTLE ARTIST

264. TWO CLOWNS

216

263. THE LITTLE ARTIST

Vallauris, May 18th, 1956.
Format 25-1/4" x 19-1/2" (64 x 49,5 cm).
Lithograph in 5 colours.
Composition executed on transparent transfer paper
with litho crayon. Transfer to stones.
5 artist reserved proofs.
50 numbered and signed proofs.

264. TWO CLOWNS

Vallauris, March 28th, 1954. Format 21-1/4 x 29-1/2" (54 x 75 cm).
Lithograph in 6 colours, the black of the two figures
having been obtained with two passes in the press.
This litho was made with a transfer of the two clowns,
drawn with litho crayon and pen on transfer paper,
transferred to stone. The colours, indicated by the artist
on transparent transfer papers, were filled in on stone at the workshop.
This composition served as a base for a tapestry.
5 artist reserved proofs. 50 numbered and signed proofs.
Stones polished out.

Back in Paris, Picasso painted several canvasses with Eugène Delacroix's famous composition in mind. He also produced two lithographs the second of which (No. 266) was to give him a lot of work when it came to engraving the stone.

1st state.

266. WOMEN OF ALGIERS. 2nd variation.

2nd state.

265. WOMEN OF ALGIERS IN THEIR FLAT
(after Delacroix) 1st variation.

265.WOMEN OF ALGIERS IN THEIR FLAT
(after Delacroix) 1st variation.

Paris, January 20th, 1955.
Format 11" x 13-3/4" (28 x 35 cm).
Composition made with an engraving-needle on a blackened litho stone.
5 artist reserved proofs.
Stone preserved.

266. WOMEN OF ALGIERS. 2nd variation.

Paris, February 5th, 1955.
Format 9-1/4" x 13-1/4" (23,5 x 34 cm).
Second version of this composition on a smaller stone; four states are made.
The stone is very deeply engraved and litho crayon scumbles appear in the 3rd and 4th states.
5 artist reserved proofs for each state.
Stone preserved.

3rd state.

266. WOMEN OF ALGIERS. 2nd variation.

4th state.

267. THE CANNES STUDIO

218

267. THE CANNES STUDIO

Cannes, November 13th, 1955.
Format 14-1/2" x 19-3/4" (36,5 x 50 cm).
Litho crayon composition on transfer paper
transferred to stone.
Background yellow ochre under the drawing.
5 artist reserved proofs.
50 numbered and signed proofs.

268. COVER FOR A CATALOGUE

268. COVER FOR A CATALOGUE

Cannes, April 1956.
Format 14-1/4" x 12" (36 x 30,5 cm).
Lithograph in 4 colours executed on transparent
transfer paper. Composition transferred to stone.
A run of 1,000 copies has been made for the cover
of the plaquette edited on the occasion of the
exposition "Dessins d'un demi-siècle"
("Half a century drawings")
at the Berggruen and Cie Gallery in Paris.

269. IN PICASSO'S STUDIO

270. FAUN

220

269. IN PICASSO'S STUDIO

Cannes, November 13th, 1955.
Format 22" x 14-1/4" (56 x 36,5 cm).
Composition in 6 colours, same process as for
the preceding numbers, realized for the book cover
"Dans l'Atelier de Picasso" ("In Picasso's Studio")
of Jaime Sabartès. Fernand Mourlot, Publisher.
Run of 250 copies. 50 copies on Japan Hodomura
paper for the follow up reserved for the first 50 copies.

270. FAUN

Cannes, April 7th, 1956.
Format 9-1/4" x 10-1/2" (23,5 x 27 cm).
Lithograph in 4 colours, same process as for
the preceding numbers.
This composition was produced
for the book cover "Dans l'Atelier de Picasso",
("In Picasso's Studio")
Fernand Mourlot, Publisher. Run of 250 copies.
50 copies on Japan Hodomura paper
for the follow up reserved for the first 50 copies.

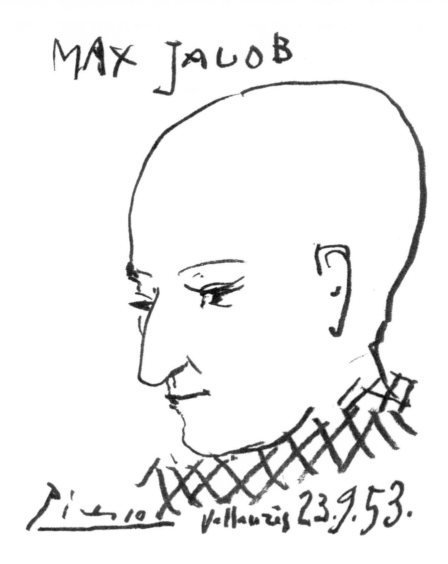

271. PORTRAIT OF MAX JACOB

271. PORTRAIT OF MAX JACOB

Vallauris, 1953
Format 6-3/4" x 9" (17,5 x 23 cm).
Lithograph executed on transfer paper transferred
to stone. It serves as a frontispiece to the book
"Chronique des temps héroïques"
("Chronicles of the Age of Heroes"), of Max Jacob,
format 7" x 9-1/2" (18 x 24 cm),
which also comprises three original dry-points.
Printing of book :
3 copies on ancient Japan paper.
170 copies on Montval laid paper.

The 30 first copies comprise moreover
a frontispiece proof on Japan paper.

Printing of engravings with margins:
8 copies on ancient Japan paper numbered from
1 to 8. 85 copies on India paper counter-sized on
Rives paper numbered from 1 to 75 and from 1 to X.
These 93 copies are signed by the artist.
For this book the artist has also executed,
on transfer paper, two lithographs in black and red
which constitute two small decorations destined
for the case packing and for the cover. (Desjobert,
printer in Paris). Louis Broder, Publisher, 1956.

272. PORTRAIT OF A WOMAN II

After a fairly long pause in his lithographic work, Picasso came across a few sheets of transfer paper and produced these four compositions which were drawn in the space of two days - a good start to the year. It should be noted that Picasso rarely produces a single lithograph; when he gets to work he normally turns out a set of several plates.

222

272. PORTRAIT OF A WOMAN II

Cannes 1955. Format 15" x 25-1/4" (38 x 64 cm).
Litho crayon composition on transfer paper
transferred to stone. A few artist reserved proofs.
50 numbered and signed proofs.

273. TWO WOMEN ON THE BEACH

274. TWO SQUATTING WOMEN

275. SQUATTING WOMAN WITH RAISED ARM

273. TWO WOMEN ON THE BEACH

Cannes, 1956.Format 18-1/2"x24-1/4" (47x61,5 cm).
Crayon lithograph on transfer paper.
A few artist reserved proofs.
50 numbered and signed proofs.

274. TWO SQUATTING WOMEN

Cannes, 1956. Format 17-1/4"x21-1/2" (44x55 cm).
Crayon lithograph on transfer paper.
A few artist reserved proofs.
50 numbered and signed proofs.

275. SQUATTING WOMAN WITH RAISED ARM

Cannes 1956. Format 16-3/4"x23-1/2" (43x60 cm).
Crayon lithograph on transfer paper transferred to stone.
A few artist reserved proofs.
50 numbered and signed proofs.

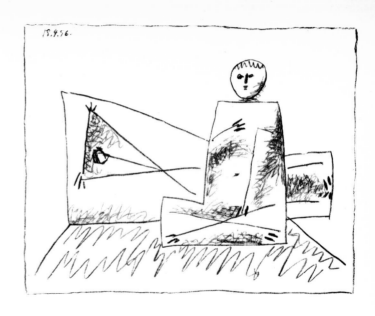

277. RECLINING MAN AND SQUATTING WOMAN

278. SEATED FIGURE AND RECLINING FIGURE

276. THE WOUNDED TOREADOR

276. THE WOUNDED TOREADOR

Cannes, 1956. Format 14-1/4" x 18-1/2" (36 x 47 cm).
Litho crayon drawing transferred to stone.
50 numbered and signed proofs.
A few artist proofs.

277. RECLINING MAN AND SQUATTING WOMAN

Cannes, 1956. Format 16-1/2" x 19-3/4" (42 x 50 cm).
Crayon lithograph on transfer paper transferred to stone.
50 numbered and signed proofs.
A few artist proofs.

278. SEATED FIGURE AND RECLINING FIGURE

Cannes 1956. Format 16-1/4" x 20-1/2" (41,5 x 52 cm).
Variant of the preceding plate.
Crayon lithograph on transfer paper transferred to stone.
50 numbered and signed proofs.
A few artist proofs.

279. THE CANNES STUDIO

Cannes 1956. Format 12-1/2" x 17-1/4" (31,5 x 44 cm).
Lithograph in six colours executed to serve as a frontispiece for the book
"Dans l'Atelier de Picasso", ("In Picasso's studio")
text by Jaime Sabartès. Book format 12-1/2" x 17-1/2" (31,5 x 44 cm)
the realization of which has taken over ten years, is published in 1957
and comprises within the body of the book the six following original lithographs :
Composition in three colours (No. 57). March 11th, 1947.
The knife and the apple (No. 78). March 11th, 1947.
The small bunch of grapes (No. 79). March 14th, 1947.
In Picasso's studio (No. 269). November 13th, 1955.
Faun (No. 270). April 7th, 1956.
The Cannes studio (No. 279). April 7th, 1956.
250 copies on Arches wove paper.
A follow up of 50 copies on Japan Hodomura paper goes with the volumes
numbered from 1 to 50 and comprises, in addition to the six lithographs above
indicated, seven lithographs reserved for that follow up, that is to say :
Composition, 3rd state (No. 32). February 18th, 1946.
Composition with glass and apple, 3rd state (No. 33). February 18th, 1946.
Apples, glass and knife (No. 76). March 11th, 1947.
Composition with stemmed glass (No. 77). March 12th, 1947.
The cup and the apple (No. 91). April 21st, 1947.
The small pot of flowers (No. 92). April 21st, 1947.
Flowers in a glass No. 5. (No. 97). April 22nd, 1947.
None of the lithographs has been signed. A few artist proofs.
Fernand Mourlot, Publisher.

280. BACCHANAL

281. THE DANCE

280. BACCHANAL

Cannes, 1956.
Format 12-1/2" x 20-1/4" (32 x 51,5 cm).
Crayon lithograph on transfer paper transferred
to zinc which served as cover for the IIIRd volume
of the 4 volume edition "Picasso lithographs",
November 13th, 1955,
in format 9-1/2" x 12-1/2" (24,5 x 32 cm).
Run of 3,000 copies on wove paper.
A few artist proofs.
André Sauret, Publisher.

281. THE DANCE

Cannes, 1956. Format 7" x 7-1/2" (18 x 19,5 cm).
Lithograph in four colours.
Each colour has been brought on transparent
litho paper with litho crayon, in register.
Used as frontispiece to the IIIRd volume
of the four volume edition of "Picasso lithographs",
November 12th, 1955, in format
9-1/2" x 12-1/2" (24,5 x 32 cm). Run of 3,000 copies.
A few artist proofs. André Sauret, Publisher.
This composition was used to decorate plates for
an edition sold for the benefit of social institutions.

282. OWL, GLASS AND FLOWER

282. OWL, GLASS AND FLOWER

Cannes, 1956. Format 17-1/4" x 25-1/2" (44 x 65 cm).
2nd state, final state.
Lithograph in six colours (the violet has been passed twice)
to serve as a poster for an Exhibition of Picasso works
at the Galerie 65 at Cannes. August 1956.
A few trial proofs of the 1st state exist;
small corrections were made to these first proofs.
2,000 copies of the poster were printed.
100 copies numbered and signed printed on Arches wove paper.
A few artist proofs. Galerie 65, Publisher.

283. THE FAUN AND THE CHILD

284. FAUN AND SAILOR or MEDITERRANEAN

283. THE FAUN AND THE CHILD

Cannes, 1956.
Format of the subject 3-1/4" x 4-3/4" (8,5 x 12 cm).
Lithograph executed to serve as a cover
for the catalogue of the Galerie 65 Exhibition.
This composition however was not utilized
and was replaced by lithograph No. 284
A few artist proofs.

284. FAUN AND SAILOR or MEDITERRANEAN

Cannes 1956. Format 3-1/4" x 4-3/4" (8,5 x 12 cm).
Lithograph in four colours.
Served as a catalogue cover for the Gallery 65 Exhibition.
This small lithograph is also called "Mediterranean".
Run of the catalogue : 1,500 copies.
50 copies with margins numbered and signed
on ancient Japan paper.
On these 50 copies has been left the indication by Picasso
in Roman numerals of the four colours utilized.
A few artist proofs. Gallery 65, Publisher, Cannes.

285. THE TUMBLERS

286. ANTIQUE SCENE

285. THE TUMBLERS

Cannes, 1958. Format 6-3/4" x 8-1/2" (17 x 21,5 cm).
Crayon lithograph on transfer paper transferred to stone.
Served as a frontispiece to Léon Level's book,
"Souvenirs d'un collectionneur"
(Reminiscences of a collector).
Format 8-3/4" x 11" (22,5 x 28 cm).
Run of 100 copies with a second litho proof on
Arches paper. 2,000 copies on Lourmarin wove paper.
Moreover 100 copies with margins on Arches wove paper
numbered and signed were printed.
A few artist proofs. Alain C. Mazo, Publisher, 1959.

286. ANTIQUE SCENE

Cannes, 1956.
Format 13-3/4" x 17-3/4" (35 x 45 cm).
Crayon and pen on transfer paper
transferred to stone.
50 copies numbered and signed.
A few artist proofs.

287. PORTRAIT OF LEON TOLSTOI

287. PORTRAIT OF LEON TOLSTOI

Cannes, 1956. Format 6" x 8-3/4" (15 x 22 cm).
Litho crayon lithograph on transfer paper laid
on a wooden board and transferred to stone.
This composition served as a frontispiece for the book
"La Guerre et la Paix" ("War and Peace") by Léon Tolstoï.
Collection "Grands Prix des Meilleurs Romans Etrangers"
Format 6-1/4" x 8-3/4" (16 x 22 cm).
Run of 300 copies on Arches wove paper
with an additional litho proof on India paper.
3,000 copies on Arches wove paper.
A few artist proofs. André Sauret, publisher.

28.11.56.

289. JACQUELINE'S PORTRAIT

4.12.56

288. THREE COLOUR PROFILE

288. THREE COLOUR PROFILE

Cannes, November 1956.
Format 16-1/2" x 20" (42 x 51 cm).
Three colour litho on transfer paper.
50 numbered and signed proofs.
A few artist proofs.

289. JACQUELINE'S PORTRAIT

Cannes, December 1956.
Format 15" x 20-1/2" (38,5 x 52 cm).
Lithograph No. 288 was made for a poster
for the Picasso Exhibition : "Un demi-siècle
de livres illustrés" ("Half a century of illustrated books").
Matarasso Gallery, Nice.
December 21st, 1956, January 31st, 1957.
At the last moment, the artist began again and
executed a second magnificient portrait of
Jacqueline, also in three colours. Picasso worked
right side out, with litho crayon, on three zincs

which were brought to him by Matarasso. At that time,
I was away from Paris. The run was executed,
in an excellent manner by the printer Berto,
at Marseilles, on offset press, which explains
why the image and the date are on the right side,
when, on a litho run the printing would be
on the reverse side. It does not alter the fact that
this is original work of great quality. Run of the poster :
500 copies., 100 proofs signed by the artist, of which 15
on Montval paper, numbered from 1 to 15,
85 proofs on Arches paper numbered from 16 to 100.
A few artist proofs on Richard de Bas paper
of various colours. H. Matarasso, Publisher.

290. COLLECTION OF SMALL PICTURES

290. COLLECTION OF SMALL PICTURES

232

290. COLLECTION OF SMALL PICTURES

Cannes, December 1956.
Format 19-1/4" x 25-1/2" (49 x 65 cm).
Composition on transfer paper in two colours.
First proof forwarded to the artist who sent it back
with the corrections indicated with a colour pencil.

290. COLLECTION OF SMALL PICTURES

Cannes, December 1956.
Format 19-1/4" x 25-1/2" (49 x 65 cm).
The tints of blue and red have been exactly followed
and the pass for press has been obtained.
It will be noted that the four reference crosses
in each corner as well as figures I and II
have been done away with on the final run.
50 numbered and signed proofs.
A few artist proofs.

292. BACCHANAL

293. THE BULL-FIGHTING GAME

291. THE FAUNS DANCE

291. THE FAUNS DANCE

Cannes, 1957.
Format 20-1/2" x 16-1/4" (52 x 41 cm).
Lithograph on zinc.
This composition was published for the benefit
of the newspaper "Le Patriote" at Nice.
200 numbered and signed proofs on Arches paper.
1,000 proofs on wove paper, signed on the zinc,
outside the composition, in the lower right part.
For these proofs a light ochre background
was printed under the composition.
A few artist proofs.

292. BACCHANAL

Cannes, 1957. Format 28" x 21" (71 x 53 cm).
Composition with litho crayon on zinc.
50 numbered and signed proofs.
A few artist proofs.

293. THE BULL-FIGHTING GAME

Cannes, 1957. Format 28" x 21" (71 x 53 cm).
Composition with litho crayon on zinc.
50 numbered and signed proofs.
A few artist proofs.

295. PORTRAIT OF D.H. KAHNWEILER I

294. JACQUELINE IN PROFILE

234

294. JACQUELINE IN PROFILE

Cannes, 1957. Format 17-3/4" x 24-1/2" (45 x 62 cm).
Lithograph with litho crayon on zinc.
On these proofs, one can see a kind of veiling on certain parts
of the sheet (it does not appear very much in our
reproduction). Probably unsatisfied with a first
portrait the artist has washed out
this image with benzine and re-worked it;
this is what explains the light grey tints which can be
seen. 50 numbered and signed proofs.
A few artist proofs.

295-296-297. PORTRAITS OF D.H. KAHNWEILER

Cannes, June 3rd, 1957. These three portraits, all striking resemblances
have been drawn with litho crayon on transfer paper.
These papers have been fixed on a wooden board, which explains
the vertical stripes in the composition, particularly in No. 295.

295. PORTRAIT OF D.H. KAHNWEILER I

Cannes, 1957. Format 19-1/2" x 25-1/4" (49,5 x 64,5 cm).
50 numbered and signed proofs. A few artist proofs.

296. PORTRAIT OF D.H. KAHNWEILER II

297. PORTRAIT OF D.H. KAHNWEILER III

296. PORTRAIT OF D.H. KAHNWEILER II

Cannes, 1957.
Format 19-1/2" x 25-1/2" (49,5 x 65 cm).
50 numbered and signed proofs.
A few artist proofs.

297. PORTRAIT OF D.H. KAHNWEILER III

Cannes, 1957. Format 19-1 4" x 25" (49 x 64 cm).
50 numbered and signed proofs.
A few artist proofs.

298 CATALOGUE COVER

299. POSTER FOR
THE 1957 EXHIBITION

236

298. CATALOGUE COVER

Cannes, 1957. Format 5" x 6-1/4" (12,5 x 16 cm).
Composition in four colours with lithographic
crayon, transferred to stone, for the cover
of the Picasso Exhibition : "Peintures 1955-1956",
("Paintings 1955-1956") at the Louise Leiris Gallery,
March-April 1957.
4,000 copies on wove paper. No de luxe printing.
A few artist proofs.

299. POSTER FOR THE 1957 EXHIBITION

Cannes, 1957.
Format 14-1/2" x 20-1/2" (37 x 52 cm).
Lithograph on transfer paper, in three colours.
Used as a poster for the Picasso Exhibition
"Peintures 1955-1956" at the Louise Leiris
Gallery in 1957. The text of this poster
has not been executed in original lithograph,
but has been drawn by the artist on a proof
and printed in photolithography. 1,500 posters
on wove paper, 25 proofs of the lithograph
on Arches paper reserved for the artist.

300. COMPOSITION

301. POSTER FOR THE CERET MUSEUM

237

300. COMPOSITION

Cannes, 1957.
Format 14-1/2" x 23-1/2" (37 x 60 cm).
This composition, in three colours,
on transfer paper was produced for Swedish
friends for the benefit of a charitable society
and sold in the Scandinavian countries.
200 numbered copies.

301. POSTER FOR THE CERET MUSEUM

Cannes, 1957.
Format 18-1/2" x 25-1/4" (47 x 64 cm).
Lithograph drawn on lithographic paper
transferred to stone for an Exhibition
at the Céret Modern Art Museum.
Run of the poster 500 copies on wove paper.
100 copies on Arches paper,
numbered and signed by the artist who,
with a colour pencil hand coloured a few proofs.
A few artist proofs.

302. THE SMALL BULL-FIGHT

303. BULL-FIGHT

238

302. THE SMALL BULL-FIGHT

Cannes, 1957.
Format 7-3/4" x 11-1/2" (20 x 29 cm).
Lithograph in four colours, executed for the review
"XXème siècle" ("XXth Century")
No. 10, March 1958.
Run 2,000 copies on wove paper.
Separate reprint with margins.
50 numbered and signed copies.
Revue "XXème siècle", Publisher.

303. BULL-FIGHT

Cannes, 1957.
Format 18-1/4" x 24" (46,5 x 61 cm).
Composition in seven colours on lithographic
papers transferred to stone : yellow, green, light blue
dark blue, vermilion red, purple and black.
50 numbered and signed proofs.
A few artist proofs.

304. THE HORSEWOMAN AND THE CLOWNS

304. THE HORSEWOMAN AND THE CLOWNS

304. THE HORSEWOMAN AND THE CLOWNS

Cannes, 1957-1961. Format 19-3/4" x 25-1/2" (50 x 65 cm).
Lithograph on transfer papers transferred to zinc,
for the first state. This composition, in red and green,
was dated November 28th, 1957. The result,
did not satisfy the artist; he took back
his zincs the following month and retouched them
on December 13th, 1957. Still not very satisfied,
Picasso abandoned the zincs for more than three
years and on March 6th, 1961, a black was made
on transfer paper. The pass for press was then obtained.
50 numbered and signed copies. A few artist proofs.

304. THE HORSEWOMAN AND THE CLOWNS

Transfer of the red, *1st state*, November 28th, 1957.
Transfer of the green, *1st state*, November 28th, 1957

304. THE HORSEWOMAN AND THE CLOWNS

304. THE HORSEWOMAN AND THE CLOWNS

304. THE HORSEWOMAN AND THE CLOWNS

1st state. November 28th, 1957.

304. THE HORSE-WOMAN AND THE CLOWNS

Zinc of red retouched. *2nd state*.
December 13th, 1957.

304. THE HORSEWOMAN AND THE CLOWNS

304. THE HORSEWOMAN AND THE CLOWNS

304. THE HORSEWOMAN AND THE CLOWNS

Zinc of green retouched. *2nd state*.
December 13th, 1957.

304. THE HORSEWOMAN AND THE CLOWNS

Transfer of the black, March 6th, 1961.

304. THE HORSEWOMAN AND THE CLOWNS

304. THE HORSEWOMAN AND THE CLOWNS

Final state. March 6th, 1961.
Format 19-3/4" x 25-1/2" (50 x 65 cm).
50 numbered and signed proofs.
A few artist proofs.

305. VASE WITH FLOWERS

243

305. VASE WITH FLOWERS

Cannes, 1957.
Format 17-" x 24-3/4" (43,5 x 63 cm).
Composition in ten colours on transparent
transfer papers. This lithograph,
executed on December 7th, 1957,
was not printed until 1961, Picasso having been
very exacting for the accurate tint of the colours.
He wanted the trial proofs begun again three times,
and for a very long period he did not give
the pass for press. 50 numbered and signed proofs.
A few artist proofs.

*This is a series of portraits on zinc,
begun on December 16th, 1957,
which Picasso considered
of great importance.
Several states of each of these plates
produced some remarkable proofs.*

1st state

306. BUST IN PROFILE

306. BUST IN PROFILE

Cannes 1957.
Format 19-1/4″ x 25-1/4″ (49 x 64 cm).
1st state. December 16th, 1957 :
composition with lithographic wash drawing on
zinc, drawing engraved with a needle in the face.
50 numbered and signed proofs.
A few artist proofs.

3rd state

2nd state

306. BUST IN PROFILE

306. BUST IN PROFILE

2nd state. January 11th, 1958.
No printing of this state was executed.

245

306. BUST IN PROFILE

3rd state, final state. December 27th, 1958.
No printing of this state was executed.
Zinc preserved.

1st state

307. WOMAN WITH FLOWER BODICE

307. WOMAN WITH FLOWER BODICE

2nd state

246

307. WOMAN WITH FLOWER BODICE

Cannes, December 17th, 1957.
Format 18-1/2" x 24-3/4" (47 x 63 cm).
1st state. Composition with wash drawing on zinc;
the date is indicated with crayon.
50 numbered and signed proofs.
A few artist proofs.

307. WOMAN WITH FLOWER BODICE

Cannes, February 1st, 1958.
Format 19" x 24-3/4" (48 x 63 cm).
2nd state. Wash drawing crayon added to the
1st state, scrapings in the bodice.
No printing of this state was executed.

3rd state.

307. WOMAN WITH FLOWER BODICE

*The zincs for this series of portraits travel
backwards and forwards between
Paris and Cannes to meet
the artist's requirements.
The No. 310 "Portrait of Jacqueline,
right profile" has become
completely unrecognizable
between the 1st and the 3rd state.
It must be stressed that this is really the
same zinc which has been utilized
for the 3 successive states.
On the evening of December 27th, 1958,
Picasso probably had a painful right
hand, as it is very hard to engrave
the zinc, especially with
the makeshift tool he probably used.*

247

307. WOMAN WITH FLOWER BODICE

Cannes, December 27th, 1958.
3rd state, final state.
Format 19" x 24-3/4" (48 x 63 cm).
50 numbered and signed proofs.
A few artist proofs.

308. BUST WITH CHECK CLOTH BODICE

1st state

2nd state

308. BUST WITH CHECK CLOTH BODICE

248

308. BUST WITH CHECK CLOTH BODICE

Cannes, December 18th, 1957.
Format 17-1/4" x 22" (44 x 56 cm).
1st state. Crayon composition on zinc. 50 numbered
and signed proofs. A few artist proofs.

308. BUST WITH CHECK CLOTH BODICE

Cannes, December 27th, 1958.
Format 17-1/4" x 22" (44 x 56 cm).
2nd state. Crayon marks added and scrapings with needle.
50 numbered and signed proofs. A few artist proofs.

309. JACQUELINE READING

2nd state

2nd state

309. JACQUELINE READING

1st state

249

309. JACQUELINE READING

Cannes, December 18th, 1957.
Format 17-1/4" x 21-2/4" (44 x 55,5 cm).
1st state. Composition with wash drawing and
crayon on zinc. 50 numbered and signed proofs.
A few artist proofs.

309. JACQUELINE READING

Cannes, January 11th, 1958.
Format 17-1/4" x 21-3/4" (44 x 55,5 cm).
2nd state. Wash drawing and scrapings.
No printing of this state.

3rd state

309. JACQUELINE READING

1st state

310. WOMAN WITH CHIGNON

250

309. JACQUELINE READING

Cannes, December 27th, 1958.
Format 17-1/4" x 21-3/4" (44 x 55,5 cm).
3rd state. Final state.
Crayon and wash drawing added,
drawing with needle.
50 numbered and signed proofs.
A few artist proofs.

310. WOMAN WITH CHIGNON

Cannes, December 28th, 1957.
Format 17-1/4" x 21-1/2" (44 x 55 cm).
1st state. Lithographic crayon composition on zinc.
50 numbered and signed proofs.
A few artist proofs.

2nd state

310. PORTRAIT OF JACQUELINE, RIGHT PROFILE

310. PORTRAIT OF JACQUELINE, RIGHT PROFILE

3rd state

310. PORTRAIT OF JACQUELINE,
RIGHT PROFILE

Cannes, January 31st, 1958.
Format 17-1/4" x 21-3/4" (44 x 55,5 cm).
2nd state. The first state called
"Woman with chignon" is completely changed,
the composition is transformed
by wash drawing solid flats and scrapings.
No printing of this state.

310. PORTRAIT OF JACQUELINE,
RIGHT PROFILE

Cannes, December 27th, 1958.
Format 17-1/4" x 21-3/4" (44 x 55,5 cm).
3rd state. Final state.
If one compares the three states
of this lithograph one realizes the wonderful
work executed on zincs and its successful execution.
50 numbered and signed proofs.
A few artist proofs.

311. BUST OF WOMAN WITH WHITE BODICE

311. JACQUELINE IN PROFILE

311. BUST OF WOMAN WITH WHITE BODICE

Cannes, December 17th, 1957.
Format 19-3/4" x 27" (50 x 69 cm).
1st state. Wash drawing composition on zinc.
50 numbered and signed proofs.
A few artist proofs.

311. JACQUELINE IN PROFILE

Cannes, March 7th, 1958.
The artist has again taken the preceding zinc
with a view to modifying it. No proofs of this state.
Cannes, December 27th, 1958.
The artist re-works the zinc a third time.
The name of the lithograph is changed.
Only a few artist reserved proofs for this 3rd state.
Zinc preserved.

CERAMIC EXHIBITION

312. CATALOGUE COVER

312. CATALOGUE COVER

Cannes, 1958.
Format 5-3/4" x 8-3/4" (15 x 22 cm).
Lithograph in two colours to serve as a cover
for the catalogue of Picasso's Ceramic Exhibition.
1,000 copies on wove paper.
A few artist proofs.
Maison de la Pensée française. March-June, 1958.

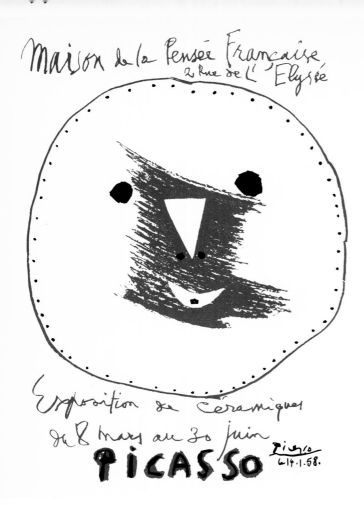

313. CERAMIC EXHIBITION POSTER

314. CERAMIC EXHIBITION POSTER

313. CERAMIC EXHIBITION POSTER

Cannes, 1958.
Format 15-3/4" x 23-1/4" (40 x 59 cm).
Two colour composition on lithographic paper
transferred to stone to serve as poster
for the Ceramic Exhibition.
500 proofs on wove paper.

314. CERAMIC EXHIBITION POSTER

Same lithograph as No. 313,
but the third colour (green) has been added.
500 copies on wove paper.
A few artist proofs.
Maison de la Pensée Française, Publisher.

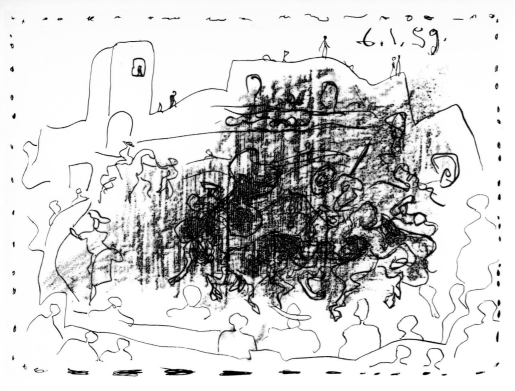

315. THE PIKE

316. JACQUELINE WITH BLACK KERCHIEF

316. JACQUELINE WITH BLACK KERCHIEF

315. THE PIKE

Cannes, 1959.
Format 19-1/2" x 25" (49,5 x 63,5 cm).
Pen composition on transfer paper,
the crayon marks have been made
with the flat of the lithographic crayon paper laid
on a wooden board, as the artist often likes to do.
50 numbered and signed proofs.
A few artist proofs.

316. JACQUELINE WITH BLACK KERCHIEF

Cannes, June 6th, 1957.
Format 19-1/4" x 25-1/4" (48,5 x 64 cm).
1st state. Drawing with lithographic crayon and ink
on transfer paper transferred to zinc. (No proofs).
Cannes, January 12th, 1958.
Format 19-1/4" x 25-1/4" (48,5 x 64 cm).
2nd state. Known under the name of 1st state.
After six months the artist takes the zinc again.
Crayon marks in the hair and in the bodice.
50 numbered and signed proofs.
A few artist proofs.

316. JACQUELINE WITH BLACK KERCHIEF

3rd state (named 2nd state). January 10th, 1959.
The zinc is "dépréparé";
crayon marks on the left hand part.
50 numbered and signed proofs.
A few artist proofs.

317. THE OLD KING

318. LORD AND GIRL

317. THE OLD KING

Cannes, 1959.
Format 19-1/2″ x 25-1/2″ (49,5 x 64,5 cm).
Lithograph on transfer paper,
executed for "Le Patriote" at Nice.
200 numbered and signed proofs on Arches paper.
1,000 copies on lighter Arches paper
with signature in red, on stone.

318. LORD AND GIRL

Cannes 1959.
Format 19-1/4″ x 25-1/4″ (49 x 64 cm).
Crayon lithograph on transfer paper
transferred to stone.
50 numbered and signed proofs.
A few artist proofs.

319. NOBLEWOMAN

320. THE GIRL WITH HAT

319. NOBLEWOMAN

Cannes, 1959.
Format 19-1/4" x 25-1/4" (49 x 64 cm).
Composition with lithographic crayon
on transfer paper transferred to stone.
50 numbered and signed proofs.
A few artist proofs

320. THE GIRL WITH HAT

Cannes, 1959.
Format 19-1/4" x 25-1/4" (49 x 64 cm).
Composition with lithographic crayon
on transfer paper transferred to stone.
50 numbered and signed proofs.
A few artist proofs.

321. THE CUP

322. THE LORD AND THE DAME

321. THE CUP

Cannes, January 10th, 1959.
Format 6-1/4" x 8" (16 x 20,5 cm).
Small lithograph with crayon on transfer paper.
Not yet utilized.
A few artist reserved proofs.

322. THE LORD AND THE DAME

Cannes, 1959. Format 7" x 8-3/4" (18 x 22 cm).
Lithograph with crayon on transfer paper
transferred to stone. Reserved for the book
"Souvenirs" de Fernand Mourlot
("Reminiscences" by Fernand Mourlot)
in preparation. Fernand Mourlot, Publisher.

323. ORIGINAL POSTERS

323. ORIGINAL POSTERS

Cannes, 1959.
Format 17-3/4" x 24-3/4" (45 x 63 cm).
Lithograph in four colours, executed for the Exhibition
"Affiches originales des maîtres de l'école de Paris"
("Original posters by Masters of the Paris School")
at the Maison de la Pensée Française, June 1959.
1,000 copies on wove paper.
A few artist proofs. There were no signed proofs.

324. THE PIKE I

324. THE PIKE I

Cannes, 1959. Format 16-1/2" x 22" (42 x 56 cm).
Litho crayon composition on zinc.
50 numbered and signed proofs.
A few artist proofs.

325. THE PIKE II

326. THE PIKE III

325. THE PIKE II

Cannes. 1959. Format 18" x 24-1/2" (46 x 62 cm).
Lithograph with crayon on zinc.
50 numbered and signed proofs.
A few artist proofs.

326. THE PIKE III

Cannes, 1959.
Format 19-3/4" x 25-1/2" (50 x 65 cm).
Lithograph with crayon and wash drawing on zinc
This plate did not stand up to the printing of proofs
and became clogged after the first proofs; owing
to this bad result, it was polished out. 3 proofs.

327. CALIFORNIAN NOTE-BOOK

1st state

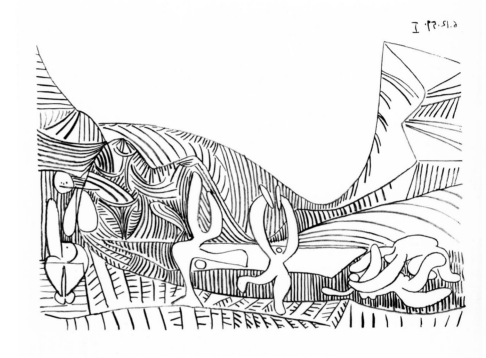

328. BACCHANAL I

327. CALIFORNIAN NOTE-BOOK

2nd state

327. CALIFORNIAN NOTE-BOOK

1st state. Cannes, November 3rd, 1959.
Format 10-1/4" x 15" (26 x 38 cm).
Litho crayon lithograph on transfer paper
transferred to zinc.
Picasso, after receiving a few artist proofs,
wants the zinc back.

327. CALIFORNIAN NOTE-BOOK

2nd state. Cannes, November 21st, 1959.
Format 11-1/4" x 15-3/4" (28,5 x 40 cm).
The zinc has been re-worked with crayon marks.
This composition was utilized for the head copies
of the "Californian note-book".
125 numbered and signed proofs.
25 artist reserved proofs, not for sale.
Cercle d'Art, Publisher.

328. BACCHANAL I

Cannes, 1959.
Format 18" x 23-1/4" (45,5 x 59 cm).
Composition with crayon on zinc.
50 numbered and signed proofs.
A few artist proofs.

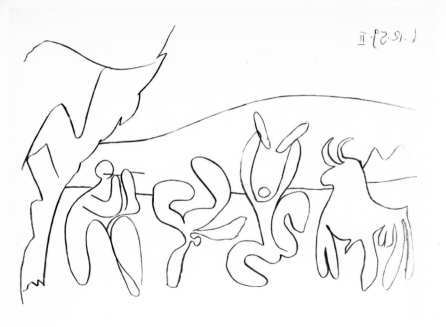

329. BACCHANAL II

330. FIGHT OF CENTAURS III

331. FIGHT OF CENTAURS IV

329. BACCHANAL II

Cannes, 1959. Format 16-1/2" x 24" (42 x 61 cm).
Composition with lithographic crayon on zinc.
50 numbered and signed proofs.
A few artist proofs.

330. FIGHT OF CENTAURS III

Cannes, 1959. Format 20" x 26-1/4" (51 x 67 cm)
Composition with litho crayon on zinc.
50 numbered and signed copies.
A few artist proofs.

331. FIGHT OF CENTAURS IV

Cannes, 1959.
Format 18-1/2" x 24-1/2" (47 x 62 cm).
Composition with lithographic crayon on zinc.
50 numbered and signed proofs.
A few artist proofs.

332. TORERO Y SENORITA

333. THE HORSEWOMAN

332. TORERO Y SENORITA

Cannes, 1966. Format 9"x13-1/4" (23x34 cm).
Composition with lithographic crayon, in two colours,
on transfer paper transferred on stone.
This lithograph to be used to complete the illustration
of the re-issue of the "Picasso-Carmen. Sur le Texte de Prosper Mérimée"
("Picasso-Carmen. On Prosper Mérimée's text"). (Bibliothèque Française, 1949).
This book will be the reproduction of a "Carmen" copy (Picasso etchings)
which the artist has enriched with wash drawings and colour drawings
for the benefit of the Centre National des Ecrivains,
and which will appear under the title "Carmen des Carmen".
A few artist proofs. Editeurs Français Réunis.

333. THE HORSEWOMAN

Cannes, 1960.
Format 19-3/4"x25-1/2" (50x65 cm).
Composition with crayon on lithographic paper
transferred to stone, executed for
the newspaper "Le Patriote" at Nice.
200 numbered and signed proofs on Arches paper.
1,000 copies on lighter wove paper,
with the signature printed on the stone.
A few artist proofs.

334. POSTER EXHIBITION 1960

334. POSTER. EXHIBITION 1960

Cannes, 1960.
Format 19-1/2" x 25-1/2" (49,5 x 65 cm).
Lithograph in black and bistre,
composed on transfer paper transferred
to stone, and destined for the poster :
"Dessins de Picasso 1959-1960"
("Picasso's Drawings 1959-1960"),
at the Louise Leiris Gallery.
1,500 proofs on wove paper.
No proofs on Arches paper. A few artist proofs.

335. WOMAN ON THE BALCONY
Poster "Œuvre gravé" 1960.

335. WOMAN ON THE BALCONY

Cannes 1960. Format 18-1/2" x 24" (47 x 61 cm).
Composition with lithographic crayon
on transfer paper transferred to stone.
Poster of the Exhibition Picasso, "œuvre gravé"
("Engraved works") at the Galerie des Ponchettes,
Nice, January-March, 1960.
625 copies on wove paper.
145 copies on Arches wove paper,
numbered and signed. A few artist proofs.

SALA GASPAR EXHIBITIONS

The five lithographs bearing the Nos. 337 to 341
have been printed in Barcelona.
Miguel Gaspar, Publisher.

336. HOMAGE TO BACCHUS

337. DIBUJOS DE PICASSO

336. HOMAGE TO BACCHUS

Cannes, 1960.
Format 19-3/4" x 24-3/4" (50 x 63 cm).
Elaborated composition, crayon, pen, scrapings,
on transfer paper transferred to stone.
This work has been taken up again six times
by the artist, as can be seen on the right
hand side of the composition, where the dates
$\frac{27.10.60}{28.30.31}$ and $\frac{1.11}{2}$ are entered.
50 numbered and signed proofs. A few artist proofs.

337. DIBUJOS DE PICASSO

Cannes, 1961,
Format 18-1/2" x 23-1/4" (47 x 59 cm).
Lithograph with lithographic crayon
on transfer paper. Poster for the exhibition
of Picasso's drawings at the Gaspar Gallery,
at Barcelona. January-February 1961.
250 proofs on wove paper.
50 numbered and signed proofs on Rives paper.
A few artist proofs.

338. CATALOGUE COVER. APRIL EXHIBITION

339. POSTER. APRIL 1961

338. CATALOGUE COVER. APRIL EXHIBITION

Cannes, 1961. Format 7"x10-1/4" (18x26 cm).
Composition in 4 colours on transfer paper.
Printing of the catalogue :
1,000 copies format 7"x9-1/2" (18x24 cm).
50 copies on Guarro paper numbered and signed.
A few artist proofs.

339. POSTER. APRIL 1961

Cannes, 1961.
Format 18"x24-3/4" (46x63 cm).
Lithograph in 5 colours.
250 proofs on wove paper.
50 numbered and signed proofs on Rives paper.
A few artist proofs.

341. ESPECTADORES

340. BARCELONA POSTER. APRIL 1961

340. BARCELONA POSTER, APRIL 1961

Cannes, 1961.
Format 21-1/2" x 28" (54,5 x 71 cm).
Crayon on transfer paper. 250 copies on wove paper.
50 numbered and signed copies on Rives paper.
A few artist proofs.

341. ESPECTADORES

Cannes, 1961.
Format 9" x 11-1/2" (23 x 29 cm).
Lithograph in black on transfer paper.
50 numbered and signed proofs
on Guarro paper. A few artist proofs.

342. PORTRAIT OF ARTHUR RIMBAUD

343. BULLS

342. PORTRAIT OF ARTHUR RIMBAUD

Cannes, 1960. Format 9″ x 11-3/4″ (23 x 30 cm).
Drawn portrait with lithographic crayon
on transfer paper transferred to stone.
Composition executed for an album "Arthur Rimbaud vu par les peintres
contemporains" ("Arthur Rimbaud seen by contemporary painters").
Nine artists collaborated in this work of format 15″ x 20-1/2″ (38 x 52 cm).
97 proofs on Rives wove paper. 7 proofs on ancient Japan paper.
A few proofs on Richard de Bas paper. All the proofs are numbered and signed.
A few artist proofs. At the expense of an amateur.

343. BULLS

Cannes, December 1960. Format 10-1/2″ x 18-3/4″ (27 x 47,5 cm).
Lithograph on transfer paper transferred to stone; this composition
was reserved for the first fifty copies of the album "Toros". This album
of format 16-1/2″ x 20-1/2″ (42 x 52 cm) printed at 500 copies on Arches
paper, comprises the reproduction of 15 of Picasso's wash drawings.
Poem of Pablo Neruda. 50 numbered and signed proofs
on Richard de Bas paper. A few artist proofs.
Au vent d'Arles, Publisher, Paris, 1960.
This lithograph was used, by transfer,
for the poster of the exhibition of the 15 wash drawings of the work,
at the Bellechasse Gallery, April 1961. 300 copies on wove paper.

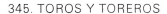

345. TOROS Y TOREROS

344. BULL-FIGHT

344. BULL-FIGHT

Cannes, 1961.
Format 12-1/2"x19-1/4" (32x49 cm).
Composition with lithographic crayon
on transfer paper transferred to stone.
50 numbered and signed proofs.
A few artist proofs.

345. TOROS Y TOREROS

Cannes, 1961.
Format 10-1/2"x14-1/2" (27x37 cm).
Lithographic crayon on transfer paper.
Composition utilized as a frontispiece
for the de luxe copies of the book
"Toros y toreros" ("Bulls and Bullfighters")
Text by Luis Miguel Dominguin.
125 numbered and signed proofs.
25 artist proofs, not for sale.
Cercle d'Art, Publisher, Paris.

6.3.61.I

346. THE PIKE. Format 8-1/4"×10 (21×25 cm).

6.3.61.II

347. THE PICADOR. Format 7-1/4"×8-3/4" (18,5×22).

A LOS TOROS WITH PICASSO

348. PASS WITH CAPE. Format 7-3/4"×10" (20×25).

6.3.61.III

349. BANDERILLAS. Format 7-1/2"×9-1/2" (19×24).

6.3.61.IV

A LOS TOROS WITH PICASSO

This album contains reproductions of 103 of Picasso's
wash drawings exhibited at the Louise Leiris Gallery,
in December 1960, showing bull-fighting figures and scenes.
Text by Jaime Sabartès.
Format of the book 9-1/2"×12-1/2" (24,5×31,5 cm).
It comprises four original lithographs produced for this work:
Nos. 346, 348, 349 and 350.
It should have included four original lithographs,
Nos. 346, 347, 348 and 349, made for this book and drawn
with lithographic crayon on transfer paper transferred to stone.

At the editor's request, lithograph No. 347 was replaced
by No. 350 in colour. Apart from the printing done for
the album, these four lithographs (Nos. 346, 348, 349 and 350)
were printed separately with margins.
André Sauret, Publisher.

A LOS TOROS

When I visited him at Vauvenargues, on April 21st,
I gave to Picasso the four lithos of the work;
at the Publisher's request, I asked our friend,
without much hope, if he would agree to put
some colours on these plates The black eyes
glanced at me and he said: "Now then! you want
some colour, Mourlot..." suspense.
"Jacqueline, show them up to the house..."
My wife accompanied me and we then followed
our hostess. The monumental staircase leads us
to the rooms, here is the bath-room, immense,
with a large green painted garden bench,
a table and iron chairs; around the washstands
a large decoration of leaves and flowers painted
on the wall by the master of the house.
We continue the visit and finally come back to
the studio, where we are invited to come in.
"You wanted some colour... here it is!"
The picador has been decorated with quite a lot
of wax pencils. I take a look at the pencil box:
twenty four colours, all have been utilized.
I am told that there are boxes with thirty-six
colour crayons...
Back at the printing works, it has been necessary
to make a tracing of each colour spot and take
the exact tint before transferring this drawing
to the stone; it is possible, although difficult,
to obtain a good result with these waxen colours
substituted for the lithographic crayon.
We have succeeded and have thus obtained this
lithograph in twenty-four colours, plus the black.
I believe that this time, it was our good friend
Picasso who was somewhat astonished.

350. THE PICADOR II

A LOS TOROS

350. THE PICADOR II

Vauvenargues, March 6th, 1961 - April 21st, 1961.
Format 7-3/4" x 10-1/4" (20 x 26 cm).
This lithograph in colour appears in the book
"A los toros" in place of the black proof No. 347.
Separate printing: 50 numbered and signed
proofs with margins. A few artist proofs.
André Sauret, Publisher, 1961.

351. FLOWERS (FOR U.C.L.A.)

351. FLOWERS (FOR U.C.L.A.)

Cannes 1961. Format 18″×22-3/4″ (46×58 cm).
Lithograph in 7 colours on transfer papers
transferred to stones.
100 numbered and signed proofs.
A few artist proofs.
This composition was utilized for the poster
of an Exhibition organized in Los Angeles
under the title "Bonne fête, Monsieur Picasso"
October-November 1961.
500 copies on wove paper.

352. THE PICNIC

276

352. THE PICNIC

Cannes, 1962.
Format 10″ x 12-1/2″ (25 x 32 cm).
Composition with litho crayon on transfer paper
transferred to stone. Was used
for the de luxe copies of the book "Les Déjeuners",
text by Douglas Cooper.
125 numbered and signed proofs.
25 not for sale proofs for the artist and his friends.
Cercle d'Art, Publisher.

THE PAINTER AND HIS MODEL

353. Mougins, 1962. Format 10-1/2″ x 15″ (27 x 38 cm).
354. Mougins, 1962. Format 10-1/2″ x 15″ (27 x 38 cm).
355. Mougins, 1962. Format 15-1/4″ x 22″ (39 x 56 cm).
"Regards sur Paris" ("Glimpses of Paris") is a book composed of
ten texts written by the ten members of the Académie Goncourt.

353. 354. 355. THE PAINTER AND HIS MODEL

Each text was illustrated with original lithographs
by a different artist. Picasso illustrated, the text of Pierre Mac Orlan
with the three above lithographs,
"Flore et Faune" ("Flors and Fauna"). André Sauret, Publisher.
These three lithographs were drawn with crayon on transfer
paper transferred to stone.
Justification of the work printing:
150 copies on Arches paper distributed as follows.
10 copies numbered from 1 to 10 with a follow up on Japan nacreous
paper, signed by the artists, and a follow up on Arches paper.
20 copies numbered from 11 to 30 with a follow up on Arches paper.
120 copies numbered from 31 to 150. 30 copies not for sale.
All the copies are signed by the ten authors and the ten artists.

356. FOOTBALL

356. FOOTBALL

Cannes, 1961.
Format 19-1/4" x 24-1/4" (49 x 62 cm).
Composition in five colours on transparent
transfer papers transferred to stones.
200 numbered and signed proofs.
Le Patriote, Publisher, Nice.

357. SPANISH WOMAN

357. SPANISH WOMAN

October 4th, 1960. Format of the composition
20-1/2"x27" (52x69 cm).
Lithographic crayon drawing on transfer paper
transferred to stone.
Run of 141 copies on Fabriano paper
numbered from 1 to 141.
(Contemporary Graphic Art Printers, Florence)
Edizioni d'Arte - Il Bisonte - Firenze.
Stone polished out.

PICASSO 1916 to 1961 (Nos 358 to 381)

358.

PICASSO 1916 to 1961 (Nos 358 to 381)

This work consists of 24 original lithographs,
including two double-page illustrations,
the remainder being intexts and inserts,
produced to illustrate texts written by Jean Cocteau about
Picasso and collated by Pierre Bertrand for this book.
Format of the book 11″×14-1/2″ (28×37 cm).
56 de luxe copies of this book,
with suite, were printed on various types of paper
and 199 copies were printed on Velin de Rives.
Drawings in soft lithographic crayon on transfer papers
transferred to stones. Editions du Rocher, Monaco.

359

Jean Cocteau
*
Picasso
de 1916 à 1961

360

I. L'HOMME ASSIS

L'or de la glace
tourne autour

Le dompteur de muses qui attache
une casserole
au caniche de la troupe
à son tour puni
médite
un mauvais coup

11

361

Un silence d'espadrille
précède le marlou

que Mnémosyne paye neuf fois
car elle tient un compte exact
de ses filles

Rien dans les manches   Rien dans les poches
Un monsieur
voudrait-il prêter sa montre
à l'arlequin de Port-Royal

362

À Erik Satie.

Vous ne trouverez ici aucun des parallèles
qu'on a coutume de faire entre Bergson, Freud,
Einstein et l'art. Cette mode pédante passera.
Picasso, s'il est un peintre poète, est exactement
le contraire d'un peintre littérateur. Rien ne lui
semble plus ridicule que le jargon de la critique
moderne.

25

363

364

365

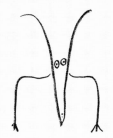

366

367

on peut se promener, qu'on peut toucher, et qui
doivent leur efficace à un rayonnement interne.
Je comptais, dans ce texte, vous parler surtout des
amis de Picasso et je m'aperçois que j'ai parlé de tout
autre chose. Mais n'est-ce pas rendre hommage à un
peintre qui a toujours pris le départ sans savoir où il
devait se rendre, et dont l'arrivée, en fin de compte,
se solde par un triomphe? Il n'est du reste pas en
mon pouvoir, ni dans mes limites, de vous dire par
quel processus le change de rythme en cours de route.
Un simple papier déchiré qui traîne par terre, suffira,
comme il arrive aux pur-sang qui se cabrent et que
le jockey cravache. Mais nous pénétrerions là dans
un domaine où l'improvisation amicale déborderait
son rôle.
Qu'il me suffise de saluer le pape, le Borgia d'une
église dont les peintres maudits, Van Gogh en tête,
furent les premiers martyrs.

368

Pourquoi me tâter le pouls ?
Vraiment je suis trop fatigué
J'aimerais mieux avoir des poux
Dans une chevelure guie.

L'urgence extrême des feuilles
Met l'automne en grand émoi.
Hiver sans que tu le veuilles
Tu dépouilles plus que moi.

65

369

Hier j'ai déjeuné avec Picasso
C'était à la brasserie Lipp
Je craignais une amère lippe
Un trou noir de palette empenné de pinceaux

Non. Un jeune chef Inca
Vint de visage si jeune
Que l'on se demandait comment le détraqua
Tout par l'orgie et le jeûne

Car lorsqu'il décidait d'ôter
Un morceau de la beauté
Il enlevait le reste et de l'autre côté.

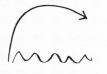

281

Excusez-moi de vous parler debout et à l'aveuglette, mais j'estime qu'il est indécent de s'installer à une table pour parler d'un homme qui invente et improvise sans cesse, d'un homme qui vit debout, travaille debout, et se trouve rarement dans la position assise.

69

370

371

372

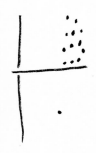

373

de Picasso est d'autant plus délicate qu'il excelle, non seulement à son jeu d'échecs, mais encore aux jeux innocents de toute sorte.

On ne saurait donc contredire ses calculs que par une innocence qui n'imite pas la sienne.

Depuis le cubisme, je regarde un cornet à surprises verser sur l'Europe : hypnoses, envoûtements exquis, dentelles en marche, insolences, épouvantails, aérogynes, ronds de fumée, perce-neige, corsets-mystère, diable à ressort et feux de Bengale.

Mais serai-je capable de voir le coup de balai prochain ? C'est le problème des fils décidant d'être des pères qui ne ressemblent pas aux leurs, et qui, une fois pères, adoptent les exigences de l'emploi. Du moins, si mes yeux baissent, mes bons yeux auront eu la chance de saluer Pablo Picasso.

374

Les yeux morts larmes d'un rire de bouche en l'air
Les cheveux blonds et la fourche fouillant les sangles
Coupant le câble extraordinaire des nerfs
Détraquant le rosier sauvage des règles

Avec des vides écœurants à force d'être
Les pleins et déliés secs de l'alphabet morse
Intelligible aux doigts aveugles des fenêtres
Et de la Vierge Noire entre l'arbre et l'écorce.

161

375

Fusillé par une grêle de raisin mûr
Une flamme de crêpe enroulée à la hampe
Écrasant la fraise espagnole contre un mur
Il allumait le soir la châtaigne des lampes.

Le double sac éjacule un flot de velours
Un solennel mécanisme de jambes roses
S'ingéniant au bout de leurs cruels détours
A ce qu'un point final agenouillé se pose.

Cette ombre singeait fausse un archange de linge
Longue langue naïve écume d'un buisson
Ardent planté de dents et du fer de l'éponge
Glaise si Picasso consacre l'écusson.

376

« Je trouve d'abord — Je cherche après. »

Cette parole de Picasso nous livre un des secrets de son génie dont il use comme d'un argent de poche. Picasso pense en actes. C'est de la sorte qu'il maltraite le visage humain à l'exemple de ses compatriotes lorsqu'ils insultent passionnément la Madone.

107

377

378   379   380   381

Picasso est suivi d'un cortège d'objets qui lui obéissent comme les animaux à Orphée. J'aimerais le représenter sous cette apparence. Chaque fois qu'il cerôle un objet il l'oblige à prendre une forme qui le rende méconnaissable aux yeux de l'habitude.

111

des champs, la clef des songes, ouvert la porte sur les surprises de la découverte.

C'est ce présent inestimable de la liberté qui lance la police contre l'audace, comme si ses entreprises étaient des bagnards en fuite. C'est ce présent inestimable qui vaudra la reconnaissance des siècles à Picasso, soit qu'il en profitent, soit qu'ils le combattent.

382. POSTER FOR
THE ALEX MAGUY GALLERY

382. POSTER FOR THE ALEX MAGUY GALLERY

April 15th, 1962.
Format of the composition 11-1/2" x 15" (29,5 x 38 cm).
Lithograph in tree colours, drawn on transfer papers
and transferred to stones. Publisher Alex Maguy
had asked Picasso to re-draw the wording of this poster
and make it bigger. The wording read: "Alex Maguy, Galerie de l'Elysée,
69, rue du Faubourg Saint-Honoré, expose sept tableaux majeurs"
30 Mai-30 Juin 1962 (exhibits seven major paintings).
The artist refused to comply with this request.
Run of 2,000 on Vélin d'Arches paper.
No signed proofs. Stones polished out.

383. FAMILY PORTRAIT I

383. FAMILY PORTRAIT I

June 21st, 1962.
Format 20″ x 26-1/4″ (51 x 67 cm).
Composition on transfer paper transferred to zinc.
The artist made full use of the properties
of the lithographic crayon.
50 signed and numbered proofs.
Zinc polished out.

384. FAMILY PORTRAIT II

385. FAMILY PORTRAIT III

384. FAMILY PORTRAIT II

June 21st, 1962.
Format 18-3/4" x 25" (47,5 x 63 cm).
Lithographic crayon drawing on zinc,
very heavily worked on the right-hand side.
Line drawing of a young woman in profile on the left.
50 signed and numbered proofs.
Zinc polished out.

385. FAMILY PORTRAIT III

July 6th, 1962.
Format 18-1/4" x 24" (46,5 x 61 cm).
6 figures.
Lithographic crayon composition on zinc.
50 signed and numbered proofs.
Zinc polished out.

386. FAMILY PORTRAIT IV

387. FAMILY PORTRAIT V

386. FAMILY PORTRAIT IV

July 6th, 1962.
Format 17" x 23" (43 x 58 cm).
4 figures, three of whom are seated.
Lithographic crayon on zinc, line drawing.
Zinc polished out.

387. FAMILY PORTRAIT V

July 6th, 1962.
Format 17-1/4" x 22" (44 x 56 cm).
4 figures.
Lithographic crayon on zinc, line drawing.
Zinc polished out.

I went to Mougins to show Picasso the mock-up of volume IV of the four-volume edition of "Picasso Lithographs". Our friend, as ever in good form, examined every page of the book with interest.

Pinned to a drawing board, the cover illustration (No. 388) that I had come for was waiting for me. The frontispiece, however, "The Artist and his Model", (No. 399), had not been planned : it was the result of Picasso's talent and our diplomacy. When I returned the next day, the cover and the frontispiece had been successfully transferred. The usual careful work was rewarded by excellent results.

388. MOURLOT COVER IV

388. MOURLOT COVER IV

February 4th, 1963. Format of the composition
20" x 12-1/2" (51 x 32 cm).
Lithograph on transfer paper transferred to stone,
having been used for the cover of volume IV
of the four-volume edition of "Picasso Lithographs"
André Sauret, Publisher.
Format of book 9-1/2" x 12-1/2" (24.5 x 32 cm).
Run of 3,000 copies.
Stone polished out.

389. HEAD OF YOUNG WOMAN IN PROFILE
LOOKING TO THE RIGHT

This series of portraits formed Picasso's
last major lithographic work.
Although the results were remarkable,
they did not meet up to Picasso's hopes.
As these lithographs were made with
white wax, Picasso thought that he would
be able to get these drawings in the form
of resists, that is, in white on a colour wash
background. But wax is a greasy product
and it became inked with black.
The artist asked for the zincs back to make
a second state, but the metal plates are still
waiting in a corner of the Mougins workshop.

288

389. HEAD OF YOUNG WOMAN IN PROFILE
LOOKING TO THE RIGHT

Format of the composition 24-1/2" x 17-3/4" (62 x 45 cm).
Lithographic crayon drawing on zinc. 10 artist reserved proofs.

390. PROFILE OF MAN LOOKING TO THE LEFT

391. PROFILE OF WOMAN LOOKING TO THE RIGHT

289

390 PROFILE OF MAN LOOKING TO THE LEFT

Format of the composition 24″ x 17-1/4″ (61 x 44 cm).
Lithographic crayon drawing on zinc. 10 artist reserved proofs.

391. PROFILE OF WOMAN LOOKING TO THE RIGHT

Format of the composition 24-1/2″ x 18″ (62 x 46 cm).
Lithographic crayon drawing on zinc.
10 artist reserved proofs.
Very heavy colour wash.

392. LARGE PROFILE OF DARK-HAIRED WOMAN
LOOKING TO THE RIGHT

393. PROFILE OF FAIR-HAIRED WOMAN
LOOKING TO THE RIGHT

392. LARGE PROFILE OF DARK-HAIRED WOMAN LOOKING
TO THE RIGHT

Format of the composition 24" x 15-3/4" (61 x 40 cm).
Lithographic crayon drawing on zinc.
10 artist reserved proofs.

393. PROFILE OF FAIR-HAIRED WOMAN LOOKING TO THE RIGHT

Format of the composition 24" x 15-3/4" (61 x 40 cm).
Lithographic crayon drawing on zinc.
10 artist reserved proofs.

394. PROFILE OF WOMAN LOOKING TO THE RIGHT

395. YOUNG WOMAN, FULL FACE

394. PROFILE OF WOMAN LOOKING TO THE RIGHT

Format of the composition 24" x 17-3/4" (61 x 45 cm)
Lithographic crayon drawing on zinc.
Crinkled background.
10 artist reserved proofs.

395. YOUNG WOMAN, FULL FACE

Format of the composition 24-1/2" x 18" (62 x 46 cm).
Lithographic crayon drawing on zinc.
10 artist reserved proofs.

396. PROFILE OF MAN LOOKING TO THE LEFT

397. PROFILE OF BEARDED MAN
LOOKING TO THE LEFT

292

396. PROFILE OF MAN LOOKING TO THE LEFT

Format of the composition 24" x 15-1/2" (61 x 39 cm).
Lithographic crayon drawing on zinc.
Light colour wash background.
10 artist reserved proofs.

397. PROFILE OF BEARDED MAN LOOKING TO THE LEFT

Format of the composition 23-1/2" x 17-3/4" (60 x 45 cm).
Lithographic crayon drawing on zinc.
Very definite colour wash.
10 artist reserved proofs.

398. THE MINER'S LAMP

399. THE ARTIST AND HIS MODEL

398. THE MINER'S LAMP

November 23rd, 1963.
Format of the composition 8-1/4 x 10-3/4" (21 x 27 cm),
on Arches wove paper 15" x 22" (38 x 56 cm).
On lithographic paper transferred to stone.
Run of 49 signed and numbered copies.
Stone polished out.

This lithograph was published in aid of the Asturian miners.
The first five proofs were coloured by the artist with
colouring crayons. Editions du Cercle d'Art, Paris.

399. THE ARTIST AND HIS MODEL

January 11th, 1964.
Format of the composition 9-1/4" x 12-1/2" (23,5 x 32 cm).
Lithograph made on transfer paper transferred to stone.
This composition was used as the frontispiece to volume IV
of the four-volume edition of "Picasso Lithographs".
Format of the book 9-1/2" x 12-1/2" (24,5 x 32 cm).
Run of 3,000 copies.
André Sauret, Publisher.

400. THE ARTIST AND HIS MODEL II

401. HOMAGE TO GEORGES BRAQUE

400. THE ARTIST AND HIS MODEL II

January 11th, 1964. Format of the composition 10" x 7" (25 x 18 cm).
Lithographic crayon on transfer paper transferred to stone.
This lithograph was produced at the request of Fernand Mourlot
for the catalogue of a travelling exhibition, organized by the
Smithsonian Institution of Washington, 1964 - 1965, which visited
American Universities. Run of 2,000 copies on Vélin d'Arches paper.
No signed proofs.
This same lithograph was also printed for a catalogue, "L'atelier de Mourlot",
("Mourlot's workshop") at the Redfern Gallery in London in December, 1965.
Run of 1,150 copies on Arches paper.
No signed proofs. The stone was polished out after the printing of these proofs.

401. HOMAGE TO GEORGES BRAQUE

February 3rd, 1964. Format 14-1/2" x 10-3/4" (37 x 27,7 cm).
Lithographic crayon drawing on transfer paper
transferred to stone. Lithograph produced
for a special number of the revue
"Derrière le Miroir", published by Editions Aimé Maeght,
in tribute to Georges Braque after the death of the great artist.
Run of 5,000 copies on Vélin paper.
350 special, numbered copies on Rives paper.
(Imprimerie Arte). No signed copies.
Editions Aimé Maeght, Paris, 1964.

402. PORTRAIT OF MADEMOISELLE ROSENGART

402. PORTRAIT OF MADEMOISELLE ROSENGART

October 29th, 1964. Format of the composition
24-1/2" x 18" (62 x 46 cm).
Lithograph made with crayon on zinc. Note the scrapings
made with a pointed scraper, intended, no doubt,
to soften some of the shading.
Only 6 proofs were produced of this portrait,
made for his friend Monsieur Rosengart.
Zinc polished out.

403-404. HOMAGE TO H.-D. KAHNWEILER

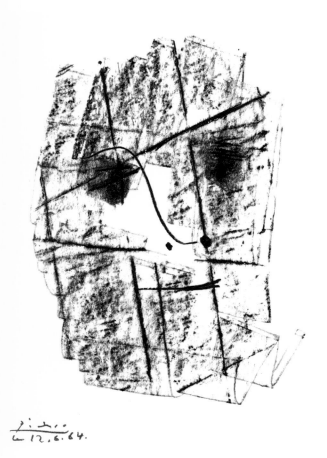

403-404. HOMAGE TO H.-D. KAHNWEILER

Work published in honour of H.-D. Kahnweiler's 80th birthday and comprising texts by his friends and original lithographs by artists connected with the Gallery.
Format of the book 11·-3/4" x 8-3/4" (30 x 22 cm).
Printing completed on December 16th, 1965, at Reutlingen, Germany.
1,000 copies were produced containing 8 original lithographs, with a 9th printed on the dust cover.
The first 200 copies constitute the original edition. Each of these included the series of 9 lithographs separately run off on

Vélin d Arches paper and signed by the artists.
These 200 copies were identified as follows:
100 copies numbered 1 to 100, intended for sale.
100 copies numbered in Roman numerals from I to C, intended for the friends and colleagues of H.D. Kahnweiler and the publisher.
Of the 9 lithographs, 2 were produced in black by Picasso:
403. The cover No. 8 10-1/4" x 6-3/4" (26 x 17), June 16th, 1964.
404 Insert No. 9 - 11-1/2" x 8-1/2" (29 x 21,5), June 12th, 1964.
These two compositions were drawn on lithographic paper and transferred to stones. Stones polished out.

405. SHAKESPEARE

405. SHAKESPEARE

February 28th 1965. Format of the composition
6-1/4" x 6-3/4" (16 x 17 cm).
Lithographic crayon on transfer paper
transferred to stone.
This lithograph was reserved for copies of the
book "Shakespeare".
Run of 125 copies numbered from 1 to 125
and 25 copies, not for sale, reserved for the
artist and his friends.
All these proofs were signed by Picasso.
Editions Cercle d'Art.

406. YEARS OF GRAPHIC WORKS

298

406. YEARS OF GRAPHIC WORKS

28 juin 1966. Format 60 x 46.
La maquette de cette affiche a été réalisée par Picasso avec des
crayons cire. Notre ami se rappelait certainement qu'à deux ou
trois reprises nous avions réussi de bons décalques.
L'affiche a été imprimée en 12 couleurs.
A la réception des épreuves, Picasso a été très satisfait et
me l'a signifié, chose assez rare chez lui.
100 épreuves sur Arches numérotées et signées.
2.000 affiches portant en haut, en caractères typographiques,
le mot Picasso, en réserve, sur fond gris. Les estampes ne portent
pas cette mention. Country Museum of Art, Los Angeles, 1966.

407. NUDE WOMAN
AND MAN WITH STICK

11.2.69.

407. NUDE WOMAN AND MAN WITH STICK

February 11th, 1969. Format of the composition
8-3/4″ x 10-3/4″ (22 x 27 cm).
Lithographic crayon on transfer paper
transferred to stone.
This lithograph was reserved for copies of the book
"Picasso - dessins 27.3.66 to 15.3.68".
Run of 125 copies numbered from 1 to 125 and 25 copies,
not, for sale, reserved for the artist and his friends.
All these proofs were signed by Picasso.
Editions Cercle d'Art, Paris, 1969.

LITHOGRAPHY

Was invented in 1796 by Alois Senefelder,
"Der Munchner", (1771-1834).
Based on the principle of the repulsion between
water and grease, the process has remained
virtually unchanged up to the present day.
A piece of limestone with a flat surface is taken
and a drawing made on it with acid-fixed
lithographic ink or with a greasy lithographic
crayon. If the stone is then moistened with a
sponge, water is absorbed by the stone which
remains wet except on the greasy part where the
drawing was made. An inked roller is passed
over the stone and the ink settles on the greasy
parts but not on the wet areas. A sheet of paper
is placed over the stone and pressure exerted.
The ink is transferred to the paper and the proof
is printed. The drawing, made mirror fashion
on the stone comes out the right way round
on the paper. To give the reader to
a better understanding of
the notes accompanying the lithographs,
we felt that it would be helpful to provide
a concise explanation of the technical terms used.

Lithographic stone. A slab of very close-
grained limestone that absorbs moisture easily.
The most highly considered stones come from
quarries in the Munich district; French stones,
which are coarser grained and less well thought
of, come from quarries in the Chateaudun region.
Cut up into slabs 2 to 4 inches thick (5 to 10 cm),
they are carefully smoothed and grained.
The graining process, which imparts the required
grain to the stone, is carried out with sifted,
moistened sandstone powder by rubbing two
stones placed face to face against each other.
The fineness of the sandstone powder used and
its abrasive quality provides a fine or a coarse
grain suited to the drawing to be made.
Smooth stones are produced by abrasion with
fine sandstone followed by pouncing.

Zinc (for lithography on zinc or, more correctly, zincography).
A zinc plate, about 0.5 cm (3/16ths ins.) thick; graining is on the same principle as for stone, but the moistened sandstone powder is rubbed on to the zinc by a heavy cast iron disc with a flat base, known as a "bourriquet", which is either powered by a motor or hand operated.

Crayon and lithographic ink.
Both crayon and lithographic ink have a base of tallow, wax, shellac, Judean bitumen, soap and lamp black. The crayon is usually in the shape of a small cylinder the same size as an ordinary pencil and is sharpened with a penknife. Intended for use on zinc or grained stone, is it used in the same way as on paper and gives a fairly wide range of effects (Picasso - lithograph No. 22).
Lithographic ink comes in the form of a small stick. Diluted with distilled water it can be applied with a pen or a brush.

Lithographic (or autographic) paper.
Grained paper sized with a substance with an adhesive paste base and gum arabic, on which the artist draws with a lithographic crayon or a pen. The paper is moistened and transferred to a stone or a zinc by pressure. The artist can work away from the stone or the zinc, but, on the other hand, the range of effects obtainable is not so great.

Transfer paper. Similar to lithographic paper but having no grain, transfer paper can be used to transfer one or several existing compositions to another stone or zinc. The original composition is inked with a greasy ink, known as transfer ink, the transfer paper is placed on the composition and a proof is obtained by pressure. One or several proofs of a single composition or of different compositions can be transferred together in a single plate to a stone or a zinc for amalgam printing.

Transferring. This operation is intended to safeguard the original composition which might become altered after several inkings and also to amalgamate several compositions meant to be printed together. It makes it possible to transfer work drawings to other stones or metal plates.

Reproduction proofs. Transfers which are not intended to be printed. These are necessary in order to reproduce a drawing in several colours. Each shade of the composition is drawn, accurately outlined and transferred to stone or to zinc. The number of reproduction proofs corresponds exactly to the number of colours to be used, each of the colours being drawn separately with lithographic crayon or ink. The reproduction proof forms the basis of the artist's design giving its outlines, rather like the outlines in a child's colouring book, but it is much finer and more tenuous and there will be no trace of it left on the final proof. It provides the guide lines for working in each colour.

Register. This makes possible the exact super-imposition of the colours. To achieve this a small cross is finely traced in the upper and lower parts of the composition; these crosses are reproduced on each reproduction proof and re-traced very accurately on each composition. The crosses are the guide lines. As each colour is printed these crosses must be lined up with great accuracy so as to obtain a good register. If this is not done the proof will be hazy and the colours will overlap each other.

Solid. Flat surface of full uniform colour or of black; it is generally obtained by filling in by brush with a good density lithographic ink.

Wash drawing. Wash drawings are made with more diluted lithographic ink. It makes possible shade effects and degrading according to the degree of dilution. Example, lithographs Nos. 88 and 68. Wash drawing produced the shaded areas on which the artist worked again with a brush to obtain the solid black and full colour parts and with a pen for the more sharply drawn parts in No. 68.

Scumbled crayon. Work that has been carried out with lithographic crayon can be rubbed with the finger, a cloth or a piece of felt to tone down, spread, or achieve a special effect, as in the top right part and the top left corner of lithograph No. 63. The artist probably placed his lithographic paper on a support with a rough surface; this roughness has resulted in some strong markings and an unusual effect.

Scumble. Light rubbing.

Gouache wash drawing. Examples, lithographs Nos. 64 and 65. On a background of lithographic ink, which is greasy, Picasso has drawn with gouache which is light. On transfer only the greasy parts remained, the parts drawn over in gouache, diluted by the moistening water, appeared as white reserve.

Reserve. Parts drawn in white or colour which appear in a dark background.

Scrapings. Scraping is intended either to lighten of to eliminate unwanted parts or to obtain a special effect. Example, lithograph No. 7. The white reserve lines in the hair and the horizontal lines at the bottom of the drawing were made by scraping the lithographic paper with the point of a knife, the hair and the background being first filled in as a solid. In lithograph No. 20 the reserve whites were obtained with a scraper. The lines are very clear cut being either very fine or very marked according to the effect desired.

Cut out lithographic paper. Example, lithograph No.1. The artist made a lithographic ink solid on lithographic paper which he cut out and transferred to stone for printing. Lithograph No. 29 bears special witness to the inventiveness of Picasso's mind. Fernand Mourlot gives a clear indication of the astute process used: lithographic paper with solid background, silhouettes cut out and worked with crayon, texts scratched in, transfer to stone for printing of proofs.

Preparation. The preparation varies according to whether a stone or a zinc is to be used. It is applied before inking with a roller and its purpose is to fix the composition and to form a coating that is not soluble in water and is water absorbent on all the parts not protected by greasy ink. It makes it possible to roller ink and run off many proofs without the composition being affected.

"Dépréparation". The aim of this is to nullify the preparation coating; it allows additions to be made (the reverse of scrapings).

This book
was produced by André Sauret _ Les Editions du Livre.
Printing was completed in September 1970
on the presses of the Imprimerie Moderne du Lion, Paris.
Lay-out, make up and typography by Claude Verne.
Composition in "univers" type by the Imprimerie Hauguel.
Photogravure by Robert Bosson, Paris.